D0913431

It's OK to Be an MK

It's OK to Be an MK

William C. Viser

BROADMAN PRESS
Nashville, Tennessee

© Copyright 1986 • Broadman Press

All rights reserved

4263-37

ISBN: 0-8054-6337-2

Dewey Decimal Classification: 266.02

Subject Headings: MISSIONARIES // MISSIONARIES' FAMILIES

Library of Congress Catalog Card Number: 86-23299

Printed in the United States of America

Scripture quotations marked (NIV) are from HOLY BIBLE New International Version, copyright © 1978, New York Bible Society. Used by permission.

Library of Congress Cataloging-in-Publication Data

Viser, William C., 1947–
    It's OK to be an MK.

    Bibliography: p.
    1. Children of missionaries—United States.
2. Southern Baptist Convention—Missions.   3. Baptists—
Missions.   I. Title.
BV2094.5.V57   1986   266'.6132   86-23299
ISBN 0-8054-6337-2 (pbk.)

To my father and mother
John and Janice Viser,
who gave me all the love a son could ask for,
taught me about Christianity,
demonstrated it in their lives,
and, best of all,
introduced me to Jesus Christ.

A Personal Word

How large is your family? Two, four, six children? Would you believe 2,677 children?[1] I would expect you to ask, "How did my family expand so rapidly?" This number represents the children of Southern Baptist foreign missionaries serving in countries throughout the world.[2] And you can be assured that the number continues to grow.

Yes, they are part of your family. In Ephesians 4:5-6 Paul reminds us that we have "one Lord, one faith, one baptism; one God and Father of us all, who is over all and through all and in all" (NIV). God is our Father, and we are His children. We are all part of His family. Nearly all of us can remember singing the chorus, "I'm so glad I'm a part of the family of God."[3]

These children are all around you today. They are coming home on furlough, they are entering colleges and universities throughout the country, and many are settling down beyond college to make their homes here.

In a sense, consider this book you family album. Within these pages, you will discover things about "your children" that you have not known before—what role they play in missions today, how the Foreign Mission Board of the Southern Baptist Convention regards them, what it is like to be part of a family overseas, adjustments to the United States, and some rather interesting programs that are being carried out by state WMUs in churches throughout our Convention as they involve MKs.

Let me tell you why I wrote a book about MKs.

1. I think they are truly a fine group. They also serve and serve proudly. You should get to know them better.

There are some misconceptions about MKs that need clarification.

3. You will be able to pray more specifically for them, their needs, and their families.

4. You will appreciate what your Foreign Mission Board does to meet their needs.

Who should read this book? It would be a misconception to think this would apply only to Southern Baptists. True, it is written by a Southern Baptist who makes mention the the Southern Baptist Foreign Mission Board, but so much of the material transcends denominational lines. Here then, are those I hope to touch.

1. I hope husbands and wives gain greater insights and feel led to become more involved in the lives of this tremendous group of young people.

2. Pastors and other church staff members should gain a perspective that will enable them to be a blessing and receive a blessing from contact and ministry with this group.

3. Young people should better understand those from other countries and establish deeper and more meaningful friendships.

4. Couples contemplating or preparing for missionary service could gain valuable insights and become exposed to various situations and dynamics, enabling them to prepare for and think through them in advance.

For the reader with special interests, let me offer these suggestions.

If you are considering appointment as a foreign missionary, you will benefit from reading chapters 1, 2, 3, 4, and 7.

If you are a pastor or church staff member, you would benefit from understanding the appointment process in chapter 2 and the attention devoted to the high school and college MK in chapters 5 and 6 as well as the Appendix.

If you are a layperson, you will find the reading in each chapter beneficial with particular attention given to chapters 5 through 7 which make extensive use of quotations from MKs and their parents. The Appendix will offer further suggestions for involvement.

If you are a teenager, you will better understand missionary kids by reading chapters 1, 2, 4, and especially chapters 5 and 6.

How do I hope this book will affect you, the reader? I hope it will touch you personally where you are, and you will become involved within its pages. There are portions that may bring tears to your eyes while others will make you laugh. Still others will be educative and will discuss areas about which you will appreciate knowing more.

What you will read will not and does not presume to speak for every MK. Each is as different from one another are we are from each other. Some MKs and their parents might not agree with certain statements. Nevertheless, reading this book will open up areas of discussion with MKs and missionaries whom you know or do not know. The result should be that you will personally come to know them better, and this is certainly my intention!

Thus, this volume is a very personal book about part of the family written to a larger part of the family.

It is my fervent prayer that God might bless and use this book to help all of us love one another more through Jesus Christ Who is love. May it serve to bring us even closer to one another as a family should be!

BILL VISER

Notes

1. The Foreign Mission Board of the Southern Baptist Convention, "MKs—Ages 1-22 by Mission, February 1981," mimeographed (Richmond: Office of Overseas Operations, 1981), p. 3. This figure changes with each year.

2. "Foreign Mission News Summary, May 14-27" (Richmond: Foreign Mission Board of the Southern Baptist Convention, 1983).

3. From "The Family of God," by William J. and Gloria Gaither, © copyright 1970 by William J. Gaither/ASCAP. All rights reserved. International copyright secured. Used by special permission of the Benson Company, Inc., Nashville, Tennessee.

Acknowledgments

I am indebted the following who helped to make this manuscript a
reality:

To hundreds upon hundreds of MKs who patiently filled out my survey
questionaires, answered this author's correspondence, spent hours
upon hours in dialogue about matters of great concern to them and
Christians the world over

To my mission family worldwide who also faithfully responded to my
survey with them providing me with a wealth of information upon
which to draw and, like their children, wrote very encouraging and
supportive remarks

To Bob Riddle and the Shades Mountain Baptist Church, Birmingham,
Alabama, who made possible the mailing of surveys to all foreign
missionaries all over the world

To my Brazilian missionary colleagues for their support and counsel

To Carolyn Weatherford, for her ever-present love for MKs and her
interest in my manuscript

To Truman Smith, senior family consultant, Family Ministries at the
Foreign Mission Board for reading the copy and making several
worthwhile suggestions

To my father, John H. Viser, Jr., my stepmother, Norma Ruth Logan
Viser, my brother, John H. Viser III, and my sister, Mrs. Clarice Gary,
for assisting me with my research and making it a family affair

To Jane Hilgenhold and Anne Baker of Truman Smith's office and to
Mary Virginia Jones and Terry Hanks, at the Jenkins Research Center of the Foreign Mission Board, Richmond, Virginia, who also
assisted in my research in so many helpful ways

To Sophia Gomes and Laura Lane for permitting me to make extensive
use of their surveys

To Vic Davis, Don Reavis, William Krushwitz, and Franklin Fowler of
the Foreign Mission Board for providing information so essential and
useful in the preparation of this manuscript

To Mrs. Vicky Bleick, Resource Coordinator of the Product Development Department for providing the photographs used within the
body of the manuscript

To the Baptist women of the First Baptist Church of Texarkana, Texas,
for inviting me to preview the book for them and providing me with
the opportunity to test the material

To my typists, Mrs. Mary Ann Lipps and Mrs. Deborah Patterson, for
their splendid work and ever-helpful comments

To my wonderful wife Susan for her ever-present support and encouragement

To my son, Ryan, for being so patient and giving his dad the opportunity to finish this manuscript

To my daughter, Lauren, who quietly sat at my feet as I wrote during
the wee hours of the mornings I couldn't sleep, and she wouldn't

All quotations are used by permission, gratefully expressed to the the
following publishers:

Alfred A. Knopf, publishers of *Personality in Nature, Society and Culture*, edited by Clyde Kluckhohn, Henry A. Murray and David M.
Schneider, "Cultural Control and Psysiological Autonomy" by Lawrence K. Frank.

Baptist Standard Publishing Company, publishers of *The Baptist Standard* for portion of " 'Missionary Kids' Feel God Calling Home" by
Norman Jameson.

Benson Company, Inc., publishers of "The Family of God," by William
J. and Gloria Gaither.

Evangelical Ministries, Inc., publishers of *Eternity* magazine for portions of "Missionary Kids Are Just Kids" by Donny Lockerbie.

Foreign Mission Board, publishers of *The Commission* for the article
"Ceremony at 15" by Leland Webb, "To the Larger Family" by
David Stewart, "Missionary Families: Some Stresses and Strengths"
by Martha Skelton, "He's Back in the Light" by Mike Creswell, "The
Shock of Coming Home" by Linda B. Kines, and "The Third World
Culture of the MK" by Franklin Fowler.

The Hogg Foundation for Mental Health, publishers of *Personality
Factors on the College Campus*, edited by Robert L. Sutherland,
Wayne H. Holzman, Earl A. Kyle, and Bert Kruger Smith.

The Japan Christian Quarterly, publishers of "A Look at the Third
Culture Child" by Ray F. Downs.

Libra Publishers, Inc., publishers of *Adolescents* magazine for portions
of "The Overseas-Experienced American Adolescent and Patterns
of Worldmindedness" by Thomas P. Gleason.

Contents

Church Member. Seven Ways of Showing Love to MKs.

Areas of Parental Preparation. First Impressions of College Life. Common Problems for MKs in College. The Ministry of the WMU; the Baptist Brotherhood; the Foreign Mission Board.

Christianity and Missionary Efforts. Their Personal Relationship to Jesus Christ. Their View of the World Today. Their Feelings Toward Those Who Support Them. Their Feelings About How Growing Up Overseas Has Contributed to Their Growth as a Person. A Word to the Parents of Future MKs. From MK to MK.

What state WMU leadership can do for MKs (Margaret Fund Students). What associational WMU leadership can do for MKs (Margaret Fund students). What local WMU leadership can do for MKs (Margaret Fund students). Requirements for adoption of a missionary kid. Adoption contract. Adoption certificate. Bylaws of the organization "Cousins." American Colleges and Universities Attended by MKs.

I Am an MK

I am a growing person, branching out from a place I know as home to a new experience in living. I continually change in this growing process, much like the cycle of a leaf from spring to fall. Inside I hold high expectations, the stuff mighty oaks are made of when they begin as acorns.

I may appear "rootless," but my heritage lies deep in the family of Christ.

I am as multifaceted as the number of leaves in a tree's covering. Also, I am as boldly truthful as the bare branches in winter.

I am not a sapling. I am strong in my convictions, and my years of experience can be counted like the rings in the core of a tree.

After maturing in my family structure like leaves in the comfort of their branches, I begin to assert myself as an individual, expressing myself as a unique human being, choosing my banner colors like the fall foliage.

After careful preparation through education and family support, I am ready to begin my journey, to be guided in God's favor toward an exciting future. Like a gentle breeze directing the path of a seasoned leaf, God's presence will direct my life.

—Susan S. Longest[1]

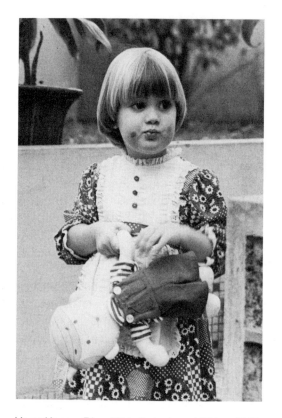

Hong Kong—Rhanki Lin Bobo is an MK too. FMB photo by Joanna Pinneo.

1
How a House Becomes a Home

Being a missionary overseas has been one of the most exciting opportunities of my life. Ask other missionaries and they will say the same thing about their experiences.

Missionaries are ordinary people doing what God has called them to do, no more, no less than what any other Christian should do in response to God's call. Missionaries and MKs do not want to be set apart and isolated as heroes or saints. They do, however, covet prayer support; and they do live in different circumstances than those in the United States.

Changes and Adjustments

As we look at family life overseas, I want to provide you with some background and share missionary Kathy Steele's burden with you.[2] She says:

The short, two and a half years we have lived as a "missionary family" have been the most stressful of my entire life.

The adjustments to a new language, different culture and new work have been difficult. We came to the field as new parents (with a six-month-old), and one year later another child was born. After the first year of language study, we moved into a country undergoing rapid change politically, socially and economically.

All of these changes and adjustments have had an effect on our lives—some positive, some negative. On the negative side,

I've seen our personalities actually change. I've thought thoughts and said words I never thought would come from within me. I've wanted to give up more times than I've wanted to go on.

But on the positive side, I know we are learning to be obedient and content in whatever circumstances.

I have noted some of the stresses we have experienced. They fall into two categories: everyday living and spiritual stress.

Everyday Living Stress

—Making out the menus for the week, then going to the grocery store to find only three of the 15 items you need.

—Never having the luxury of a nursery at church.

—Going to the drugstore to find only one of four medicines the doctor prescribed for your sick child.

—Living in terrible heat 24 hours a day. Sweating so much that your watch turns green inside. Being so hot physically that you emotionally explode at the slightest irritation or inconvenience. Going to a restaurant and paying $2.50 for a greasy piece of chicken just to sit in the air conditioning.

—Living with a spouse who is no longer himself or herself, due to all the daily stress and tension.

—Not being able to find a dress or pair of shoes big enough to fit.

Spiritual Stress

—Not understanding much of the sermon due to 1) unfamiliarity with the language and 2) your one- and two-year-olds sitting on your lap while the sweat streams down your neck and drips off your forehead.

—Spending Christmas alone.

—Not being able to share on a deep, intimate level with people due to lack of time to develop relationships and problems with the language.

—Wanting to go home, yet knowing the Lord has called you here and is working in your life to build his very character into you through the problems."

You could not place every missionary in this situation. Some missionaries might suggest other "stresses" peculiar to the culture within which they work. I share this simply that you might be more aware that all missionaries face stress in some form or another and that you might be able to pray more specifically for them.

Physical Stress

Certainly, every missionary family faces these two stresses to some extent, but there is a third stress as well that should be included. That is stress leading to physical illness illustrated in this account.[3]

Missionaries Leo and Margaret Waldrop, now more happily and healthfully serving again in Surinam, went through health crises within their family in 1980. Medical problems plus field discouragements set in:

"Because of continued lack of Dutch teaching materials and lack of personnel to cover for regular furloughs, our family had about decided to seek another direction in ministry," the Waldrops wrote.

Leo and family came home on medical leave because he had developed an ulcer. On extended medical leave and with further health problems for family members, Leo said facetiously that he "should study medicine and open a hospital. Family problems alone would keep it in operation!"

Everyone recovered, however, and Leo's ulcer subsided with proper medication and Christian counseling on how to deal with stress. They reflected joy on returning to Surinam and getting back into their ministries. "We are already seeking God's will as a possibility for starting a new church," they reported.

Within a missionary family, what happens when serious medical problems are faced? There may be competent care on the field which can meet the family's physical

needs. Another option—where this may not be the case—
is to consult Franklin T. Fowler, an MD, who serves as the
Board's medical consultant. Medical leaves can be arranged through him, thus allowing the missionary or MK
to receive adequate treatment within the United States.

Though the result will hopefully be the return of the
missionary or MK to the field, this is not always the case.
The John Pattersons, former missionaries to Columbia,
illustrate this situation.

Due to head injuries which their son received in an
automobile accident in Columbia, they found that treatment for the long-term effects was simply not available.

Patterson summed it up well when he shared his belief
that their mission field is the United States. "We did not
leave the mission field, . . . we only moved our center of
operations for doing mission work."[4]

According to recent statistics, there are 2,677 MKs from
ages one to twenty-two living on mission fields throughout
the world. The three largest concentrations of MKs are
found in: the Philippines, South Brazil, and Japan.

The Missionary Home

The missionary home is, like every other home, a great
influence upon the life of the child. Since the family and
culture are primary conditioners of the child's self-concept, an unstable home or an extremely difficult culture
can do damage to the child. The individual tends to maintain the formations of self-concept made in earlier life and
abrupt or drastic changes in the family or cultural setting
are likely to cause the individual to feel highly threatened
and disorganized.[5] This can and does happen to the missionary family.

The Role of the Missionary Father

In an article from the *American Journal of Psychiatry,*
Dr. Sidney S. Workman wrote:

> In the United States, typically, a mother cares for her chil-
> dren and knows their environment and entire range of activi-
> ties only too well. Though the involvement of fathers with their
> children in the United States varies, there is an expectation that
> fatherhood implies at least a supportive role in parental func-
> tions. Upon arriving at an overseas post, a father is often swal-
> lowed up in his career and disappears from his family,
> substantially, for good.[6]

Lucinda Shelton, an MK from Uruguay once commented that people assume everything is always great with
missionary families. She related that, "Missionary family
life is not easy. Many missionaries don't always have everything solved."[7]

Part of the difficulty within the missionary family, like
that of any religious vocational work, can be traced to the
absence of the father.

When we were in language school in Campinas, Brazil,
we were told that our primary objective was to master the
Portuguese language. We were not to jump into opportunities and assume outside responsibilities that would
hinder us from devoting our best to the language study.
Why? Whatever good we might be able to do by accepting those opportunities of the moment would forever
compromise the good we would be able to do in the years
ahead based on a good solid grasp of the language. What
this translated into was the opportunity to define our time
between language study and our family. For most of us,
it was a new experience. We were accustomed to doing
many things at the same time back in the United States.
Some handled this extremely well. They did more things
as a family. Television and radio had no claims since they

could understand very little of what was being said. Close bonds with other families were established. Families did more activities outside, picnics, seeing the local sights, and so forth. The local church and their opportunity to feel welcome and to fit in took on a new light.

Some, however, let other things creep in and take that much-needed time away from their family. I was told of a language-school student in another country who became heavily involved in his hobby of being a "ham radio operator." He spent so much time talking back and forth to the United States that the children were told not to disturb him. He suffered, his wife suffered, and the children suffered.

Others may become overly involved in language study. One missionary told me that this was his reason for being here, and he would permit nothing to interfere. He literally shut himself within a room at night to study and would not come out.

Also, there is always the temptation to become overly involved in outside activities. Perhaps the husband has a facility with the language that comes rapidly, or the language is one he studied in high school or college. The temptation is to accept numerous invitations to preach. The result is that the father is removed from the family quite suddenly at a time when all family members need quality time together to make their gradual adjustment.

Another factor in the absence of the father can occur once the year of language school is completed.

The father, let us say, has limited himself to his language study and has devoted adequate time to his family, but now the family has moved and is located in their assignment. Opportunities open up, and invitations keep coming at a greater and greater rate. The longer he serves, the more needs he sees, the greater the realization that "only I can meet them." So the personal calendar begins to fill, a day here, a day there, a weekend or two, a week here and there. Soon he is gone more than he is at home. Two potential disasters are obvious.

First, he is going to "burnout" and may collapse from physical exhaustion.

Second, he may suffer a possible nervous breakdown. This happens in missions ranks much more frequently than one might suspect. Why? As I suggested earlier—overwhelming need is so evident.

I recall a conversation early in my missionary life with a senior missionary who placed it in this perspective. The difference, he said, in needs here and the United States is that when someone calls you (or writes) in the United States and asks you to do something and you cannot, someone else can be found without too much difficulty. Overseas, if you say no, the entire event may be canceled.

This can weigh on your mind, without a doubt. On the other hand, I recall another conversation with a missionary colleague who suffered a nervous breakdown due to an impossible work load. He related that one day his doctor in the United States (where he was recuperating) asked him if he had read his New Testament lately and suggested he do so again. The doctor later asked him if Jesus had done everything that everyone asked him to do. The missionary replied no, and the doctor responded, "If Jesus did not, how can you?"

A balance must be found by each father. The often conscious factor is that the missionary may feel that those back home in the United States are expecting him to be busy twenty-four hours a day. He might feel that the busier he is and the more he is doing, the better missionary he is.

The family feels the effects of the father's frequent absences. Unless it is handled correctly, it will become like a ticking time bomb set to go off at some future date.

One MK shared with me, "Dad got so involved in work that he would set me aside worrying more about the problems of others than my own. My Dad and I had difficulty talking with each other. Mother relayed appreciation from me to Dad and vice versa."

Another echoed the same and said, "Neither one of us took the risk of trying to get close to each other. It seems that our relationship was sort of superficial all along."

Solutions to His Dilemma

What then is the answer? How can the work be done without compromising the emotional and physical health of the missionary father? How can the overwhelming needs be met without causing a temporary or permanent disruption within the family?

I believe the following would be helpful.

1. We should pray daily for our missionaries, for their spiritual discernment, their total health, their work, and their family.

2. The missionary father should see the importance of the family unit and strive to strengthen it by every means possible.

3. Quality time as regularly as possible should be planned and set aside for each family member.

4. He should remember daily that just as Jesus did not meet every need that existed, neither can the missionary.

5. He should frequently recall that those who support him in the United States both prayerfully and financially do not expect him to exhaust himself in his work, but they pray for him to have a long continued ministry where he is serving.

6. He might also remember that abusing his body physically, his mental health emotionally, or his family will eventually abuse his ministry for Christ as well.

7. He should try to involve his children wherever possible and help them to feel a part of the work.

Franklin Fowler commented on this when he wrote:

Parental identification becomes more important for a child living in a third culture with a minority group. The child who feels himself a missionary, as his parents, is fortunate to have such wise parents. They have been able to identify closely with him.

The missionary child who is allowed to accompany his parents on field trips, who in some way becomes part of his parents' work, who knows the reason for their being overseas—that child is indeed adjusted and fortunate.[8]

Of equal importance to the adjustment of the missionary family overseas is the role of the mother.

The Role of the Missionary Mother

While working on my Doctor of Education dissertation, I developed a questionnaire for MKs which I mailed to every MK enrolled in colleges and universities throughout the United States. Among the information I was seeking was what they felt to be their three most common problems and what they considered to be the source of those problems. Two hundred and thirty-four MKs responded with these results.[9]

Three Most Common Problems	Source of Problems
(1) Longing for my foreign roots	(1) Foreign culture
(2) Culture shock	(2) Absence of the mother / secondary source of education
(3) No sense of loyalty or commitment to the local church	(3) The hostile environment which may be related to the treatment received in the foreign country as well as in the United States.

As you can see under the source of problems, number two, the absence of the mother was felt keenly by the MK. The missionary mother can be every bit as vulnerable to potential disruptions in the home as the father. One of these would be the balance she will maintain between the home and her activities outside the home.

A missionary mother illustrated this dilemma.

"In my first years as a mother and on the mission field, I didn't know whether I should be a mother or a missionary, . . . I felt an obligation to be out with the people. I thought being a mother and a missionary were two different things. I didn't realize until my children were gone that they could be one and the same."[10]

Another missionary associate mother adds, "Now that my children are grown, I realize even more clearly that these children are our first responsibility. My children now in their maturity have expressed to us that there were times when they were younger that they felt somewhat neglected because we were so busy doing 'God's work.' "[11]

Many factors will determine how much time a missionary mother has to give beyond her primary responsibility to her family: the missionary field in which they serve, the age and number of the children, the existing educational facilities, and the cost and need for domestic help.

Some people in the United States have a problem when they hear of missionaries with domestic help. Visions of living in palatial splendor may come to mind. *I can't afford domestic help, how can they,* it might be reasoned.

What some never stop to consider is that the situation is totally different on the mission field. Few American housewives have to make their meals from scratch and spend hours preparing a meal that could be put together in thirty minutes in the United States. Not too many

Americans would live in a hot climate where the temperature may average close to 100° or better and not have air conditioning. This may well be the situation for the missionary mother who must leave her windows open all day with the result being a daily influx of dust and who knows what.

Many Americans fail to appreciate that the sheer simplicity of maintaining a daily schedule in the United States does not always translate in another culture. The result is that the missionary mother may find herself going to three or four different places to find the same things an American mother could find under one roof in the US. She may not be able to pay her bills by mail and has to stand in lines for an hour or more.

There are other dynamics involved in the missionary having domestic help.

First, it actually helps free the mother to be what she should be—a wife to her husband and mother to her children.

Second, there is the increased likelihood that the time saved physically and emotionally from doing chores that another can be paid to do will afford the mother more time to devote to missionary work.

Third, in some countries domestic help is very reasonable and thus enables someone who wants it to earn a living.

Fourth, it may be a means of helping some young person attend seminary or college as they help the missionary family.

The balance of time, therefore, can be seen as a matter the missionary mother must come to terms with.

Another potential disruption may be her sense of her own call. More than half of the new missionaries who attend orientation at Missionary Orientation Center

(MOC) in Georgia each fall and winter are women.[12]
More than two thirds or 69 percent of missionary home-
makers are women with a strong sense of personal call
from God to missions.[13] The importance of a personal call
cannot be over emphasized. Pressures begin to affect the
missionary family before they leave the United States and
have a habit of building sometimes subtly and sometimes
not so subtly on the mission field.

While in language study in Costa Rica, the Charles Ho-
wells discovered this. Charles relates:

> The pressure began to mount on us all. Gail could not find
> anything that suited her. The food was bad, the house dirty. I
> responded with indignation, "You knew it was going to be this
> way!" I said, red-faced with anger. "Why can't you cope with it?
> Look how well I'm doing."[14]

It is times like these in the beginning of the missionary
mother's life and further down the road that can over-
whelm her without a strong sense of calling to lean upon.

I often recall the words shared with us at our missionary
commissioning service. Winston Crawley, Vice President
for Planning, quoted Baker James Cauthen as saying,
"Sometimes the only thing that will keep you on the field
is your sense of calling."

A missionary mother may tend to devalue herself without having had a clear sense of call.

Linda Bridges, missionary to Taiwan, put it this way:

> The missionary woman does not receive her call through her
> husband, but understands that God calls her, individually, to use
> those gifts that belong to her. Neither husband or wife needs to
> forsake the responsibility of the home. This is a mutual responsi-
> bility, as the vision of ministry begins in the home and pene-
> trates beyond the community and nation.[15]

A third challenge to the missionary mother as she trans-

plants her family into another culture is to consider herself a person of worth. Some cultures can make this difficult for the mother to maintain.

One missionary couple in Brazil, veterans of several
years of service, laughingly (now) tell the story of going
out with another couple for an informal dinner. As the
men finished ordering dessert for themselves and their
respective wives, one wife suddenly changed her mind.
Rather than tell her husband, she simply addressed the
waiter with her new request. To the men's delight, the
waiter turned back to her husband and said, "Is this
change acceptable to you?"

Rebekah Naylor, missionary physician to India wrote:

> Amid tensions in a male-controlled and oriented profession,
> . . . I have found that I can be accepted as a person of compe-
> tence and worth on the basis of my character and performan-
> ce.[16]

I believe this is just as applicable for the missionary
homemaker who may find it necessary to devote more of
her time in the home.

Naomi (Mrs. Leslie G.) Keyes, missionary to Honduras,
related that a young pastor approached her and her husband prior to his marriage to ask for advice on how to raise
children. He wanted his to grow up to be like the Keyeses
children.[17]

Jean (Mrs. Bob L.) Spear, missionary to Thailand, related this thought:

"We Southern Baptist women missionaries are thankful
to a Foreign Mission Board that permits us freedom of
expression in our witness and allows us to be a person in
our own right."[18]

Perhaps a capstone on the matter of the missionary
mother's being a person of worth was stated by missionary

Wayne Fuller in Lebanon, "Without the women, this Mission would fall apart."[19]

The support or lack of support from the parents of the missionary may have a way of keeping the new adjustment in the state of turmoil or in a state of calm. Personal feelings are important to all of us. Though the missionary couple is doing what they feel to be God's will for their lives, negative parental concerns expressed in various ways can have an unsettling effect prior to the family's adjustment overseas and later on as well.

Statements such as, "Don't take our grandchildren away from us," and "You aren't going to like it 'over there,' " and "You'll be home again soon," or "Don't you know we have a real mission field right here in the US?" may often be heard.

Some parents will have the opportunity to visit their son or daughter or son-in-law or daughter-in-law overseas. Once they see with their own eyes how involved in the work and well adjusted their son or daughter and family is, they will return to the US with a new perspective.

I shall never forget an experience like this one night in Campinas, Brazil. All of the language school students and teachers were seated together in a rather large circle. We had eaten together, laughed and sung together, and prayed together. The parents of an Assembly of God couple were present. The young couple and their family were good friends of ours and well liked by the other students and the Brazilian teachers. During a quiet time of sharing, the mother of the missionary wife got to her feet, and, with tears in her eyes, said, "I am so glad that God has called my daughter and her family to a place such as this."

It was a deeply moving time for all of us, for I felt that she was saying what all parents would do well to express. Parental support can be so encouraging and lack of it, very discouraging.

Another concern for the missionary wife is learning to manage alone. It is often necessary for the husband to spend time in travel. Depending on the nature of the husband's work, some will have to travel more often than others. This means that she must care for the family and home alone. She may even find herself making some decisions in her husband's work that he would normally make when present. All of these responsibilities, best shared when both are together, can take their toll when she finds herself making them alone. This is all the more accute when she lives in a remote region with few or perhaps no other missionaries around.

A final concern I shall mention here is the education of the children. This responsibility will fall upon her for the most part. How long she will teach them will depend upon the local conditions. She may share this responsibility with several other missionary wives. The more remote their location is, the less likely that she will be able to educate her children on a shared responsibility basis. We will explore the entire educational option later in this chapter.

Single Missionaries

I want to insert a word here about another group of men and women who, though not married, certainly may exert a very wholesome influence on the settlement of the new family. They are single missionaries. From the fall of 1969 to the fall of 1981, 115 career singles and 26 associate singles—for a total of 141—have attended orientation.[20] Many more single women than single men are appointed as missionaries each year.[21] These singles will become needed members of the extended family. They, along with missionary couples, are just as capable of "spoiling" the MKs as their counterparts in the United States, and it is beautiful to see the way they develop a close-knit relationship. So close can the substitute relationship become that it may pose a problem to grandparents back in the states.

For example, I remember hearing of a missionary couple (let's call them the Clarks) whose friends (call them the Deans) had left to begin their furlough in the United States. The Clarks soon followed the Deans on furlough, and when the Clark family arrived at the airport there to meet them were their parents who had not seen them in several years and the Jones family as well. Who do you think the Clark children rushed to see first? If you guessed the grandparents, you guessed wrong! It may not be hard for you to become indignant over this, but then, when you stop and think about it, who would want to deprive their grandchildren or nieces or nephews of meaningful contact with other loving adults when they themselves cannot be there? Missionary singles and missionary couples can and do substitute here to the benefit of all concerned. When you live, eat, breathe, and share a common work as all missionaries do, you can understand why they can be such a close-knit family, and that is the way it should be!

Having examined the role of the missionary father, mother, and single missionary in the adjustment of the missionary family overseas, let's go a bit deeper into the dynamics of the missionary family life—what new aspects and concerns it takes on as well as some differences from family life in the United States.

All missionaries receive extensive orientation on the family while in Georgia. Truman S. Smith (see Glossary) and others lead these sessions.

Upon arriving on the mission field, the missionary family finds a house provided for them. It may be the only one available, or the family may be able to choose from a few vacant ones at the time of their arrival. It may be that they will have to choose suitable housing or build. The Board has specific guidelines for choosing or building a house or dwelling that the mission does not already own. The Foreign Mission Board, at its meeting on February 8, 1982, adopted the policy wherein the standard size of future mission housing must not exceed 1,600 square feet (outside measurements not including a carport). The carport itself should not be enclosed except in the event of security needs.[22]

Of course, as the saying goes, a house is not a home. Missionary family life must be cultivated. It must be something that all family members value and work together to make worthwhile.

Evidently, most do just this and succeed well.

The Tie That Binds

In her survey to college MKs, Laura Lane asked the question, "As an MK do you feel that your family has closer ties than the 'normal' U. S. Family?" Eighty-two percent responded yes, 10 percent responded no, and 8 percent were uncertain. Of interest, also, was the fact that Mrs. Lane discovered MKs who attended boarding schools still felt closer ties to their parents.[23]

In one of several surveys I conducted, I questioned the missionaries of the South Brazil Mission of which my family is a part at our annual mission meeting concerning the time aspect of their family life. I want to introduce the results with the following information:

(1) 49 percent of the respondents were males.

(2) 51 percent were females.

(3) The average age of the respondents fell into the 40-49 year age range.

(4) The average length of time spent on the field was fourteen years.

(5) The average number of children per respondent was three.[24]

The question was, "In regard to family time, I feel that we have as much, if not more, time than we had in the United States."

Sixty-four percent responded yes.

Eighteen percent responded not sure.

Eighteen percent responded no.[25]

Missionary Edgar Hallock, a veteran of forty years of service, offered this impression: "In the United States there are tremendous pressures, even more than in Brazil."

A missionary wife added, "Since there were fewer extracurricular activities in school and most outside activities were connected with the church, we did more things as a family."

Leona (Mrs. Joe) Tarry, with nineteen years of service volunteered that they scheduled a regular family night each week.

Maxie (Mrs. James P.) Kirk, having spent thirty-five years in Brazil, shared: "Our children were with us from 1948-1973. We *took* time for family fellowship and are grateful for friends who so strongly advised us to do so."

James Kirk added, "I marked out time in my 'agenda' as family time and counted it as 'sacred' as any other engagement."

Doris (Mrs. Dan) Sharpley (retired) with thirty-five years of service wrote, "When the kids were small I read three books—their choice each night before bedtime. Around the table at breakfast we had our worship time with each one using a Bible and each reading. We took turns at praying with all participating, and we still do."

We have heard from the parental side, and now I would like for you to catch an intimate glimpse from the MK perspective. Some of the comments you will read came from a survey I formulated and had distributed at an annual MK Thanksgiving Retreat. One hundred and thirty-one MKs (65 male and 66 female) representing fifty-eight different countries responded. Other comments will come from conversations with MKs while doing work on my dissertation.

As you read these personal comments from MKs across the world, I think you may better understand how MKs view their family in a foreign setting and how they see the American family.

Sally Wilson, MK from Taiwan, said, "It seems that missionary families are much closer than many American families. It's hard to get used to students being so happy to get away from their families."

Lydia Hammett, MK from Taiwan, said, "Many families are broken up in the United States. I have had a close and happy family life. It is still hard for me to realize not everyone is as lucky."

Dorothy Thomas, MK from Thailand, added, "Well, overseas the missionaries are your aunts and uncles and family. Families are so *close* . . . meeting so many kids from broken homes was one thing that freaked me out when I came to the states."

Karen Doyle, MK from Guatemala, related, "Life overseas is more family oriented. The lack of concern for family members in the United States outside the nuclear family is a real shock to my system."

Kris Spencer, MK from the Philippines, touched on a sensitive note to all parents when she shared, "We have a close-knit family overseas. Your parents *can* be your best friends."

Ten Challenges to the Missionary Family

Now let's look at ten areas confronting missionary families today.

Commonness of Circumstances

In the missionary family, everyone has to make adjustments. Everyone "starts from scratch." True, the younger the child is the less set he is mentally and emotionally, and the more flexible he is. Beyond this, however, things tend to be more equal at the outset.

The family learns quickly to "rally around one another" and provide much needed emotional support.

Stephen Law, MK from Spain, illustrates this as follows, "You depend more on your immediate family as you have no one else to go to. This reliance makes you resent your parents and their work or gives you a new understanding about it. I have chosen the latter. I have a deep respect for my parents."

I remember walking home with Ryan after his first day of Brazilian school in Rio. He very indignantly told me that the boys at school (where he was the only American) told him, "You don't have the tongue," meaning that he couldn't speak their Portuguese language. I asked him what he told them. He said that he responded to them in Portuguese and said he did have the tongue! I assured him that he did, and in no time at all you could not tell the difference between his Portuguese and his Brazilian schoolmates.

Crises can, quite naturally, serve to pull families closer together. Mary Carpenter, an MK from Indonesia, related that during a riot her father, a doctor, helped a man who was badly cut up. They later found out that he was a Communist who had been assigned to kill the family.[26] Another MK added, "Going through a revolution does wonders to family relationships."

Elizabeth Watson, MK from Venezuela, said it well when she stated, "A missionary family is more closely knitted than most. This is due to the fact that family members, especially children, depend on each other for fun, sharing and love."

Cultural Balance

As the American family is transplanted into a foreign culture, it seeks to identify with the foreign culture it is a part of and yet retain its American heritage as well. This can produce some subtle dynamics unique to the situation.

For example, American items can become much higher in value to the family simply because they are American. There is also the ever present reminder that they cannot be replaced in the country, and once they are gone there may not be access to more. For example, cherry pie filling may be rationed out as far as it can go. American candies may be parceled out a few at a time. Cans of soft drinks may be hidden away for special occasions! Silly, you say, but everyday things you have such easy access to can become all the more desireable when you *know* that you cannot get them.

This can create not only an inflated sense of value but also communicate a message to the MKs in the home as well.

One MK told me that she kept hearing her parents talk about material values to the extent that when she returned to the US to begin college, she had a desire for more than she might have without all the emphasis.

A male MK from a Latin American country told me, "They built it up so much. When I arrived in the US and tried it [ate those certain foods, etc.], I couldn't understand what the fuss was all about."

Another said, "My parents would say how thrilled they were when they sang or heard 'The Star-Spangled Banner,' I felt guilty because I wasn't thrilled."

Some MKs related that certain types of American tourists, those who show a lack of respect for local customs or make uncomplimentary remarks, had a tendency to color their feelings toward the US. Of course, it goes without saying that the attitude of the foreign country toward the US can also have a bearing here.

Several commented on American holidays.

Two MKs said they had never celebrated Thanksgiving in their home. This is difficult for many to understand, but it should be pointed out that the rest of the world does not observe Thanksgiving when we do, if they celebrate it at all. In order to hold to an entire day of celebration, children might have to miss school and the husband not teach his classes, and so forth. Of course, it could be argued successfully that, nonetheless, it could still be observed in a special way; it could and should be, in my opinion.

It is the failure here that leads some MKs to say what they have said to me, "We never really saw holidays as significant—only American—an excuse for a holiday."

It is apparent that certain events should be remembered and observed but most of all explained, if the children are to understand and appreciate them.

On the other hand, parents can tip the scales on the other end. They can insist on observance of only the holidays of the foreign country, duplicate their manner of observing them, and speak only the national language.

One MK shared with me that she knew a family that did this, and when the kids grew old enough to return to the US for college they totally rejected the US—electing to stay in the foreign country. Their adaptation went too deep due to lack of balance.

Isolation

This may occur in one of several ways.

1. Geographical isolation. A missionary family may feel God's leadership to a location where they are the only

missionaries. I have known some to delay this decision until their children were enrolled in college while others have gone with their children still in the home. This isolation affects MKs in different ways.

MK Lorrie Horton of Kenya, East Africa, said, "We were on a station by ourselves which I enjoyed. There was no television or a lot of entertainment. As a family we did much together. I found I appreciated my family more."

Another from Venezuela saw it somewhat differently and related that she was isolated from other MKs due to her father always accepting assignments to far out-of-town places. She missed this contact.

2. Educational isolation. What about the children's education? They may be taught in the home at the expense of social development (as in contact with children at school), or they may go off to boarding school. This, of course, forces the separation that all missionaries eventually face, but in this case it occurs much earlier.

One MK shared with me that he left home for boarding school in the fifth grade. Can you imagine how it would feel to have your child leaving home to go off to school at ten or eleven years of age?

I like what an MK girl from Indonesia said in regard to this kind of separation when she stated, "God really fills the gap left by parents." To be certain, His ministry strengthens not only the MKs but their parents as well.

3. Material isolation. Very few of us truly appreciate the day-to-day luxuries we have in this great country of ours, but they become sharply apparent the longer you live in another culture.

Albert McClellan put it this way:

You live in Indonesia, and your Sears, Roebuck refrigerator breaks down, what do you do? You send nine thousand miles away for a relay switch that takes six months to arrive. Or you live in Ghana where you hand pump water from a well into an oil drum storage tank, and this becomes your family's water supply for the day. Or you live in Guatemala where your meat market and grocery store are open stalls on the streets, and where there are no McDonalds or Kentucky Fried Chicken or name-brand canned goods or any canned goods you can afford.

Or you live in a country where medicine is a mixture of magic and old wives' tales and where the nearest hospital for having babies is more than three hours away, and you are told next year the missionaries cannot use it anymore. Or you live in a country where beef costs $6.50 a pound and gasoline $2.00 a gallon. Or you live under the constant threat of malaria and diarrhea. After a while refrigerators and supermarkets and even safety do not hold the values they seem to hold in America. You are anguished, but you hold on because you are a missionary.[27]

Lack of peers

A missionary family might move to a missionary station where there are numerous MKs, yet the age differences are so far apart that isolation still exists.

For example, when we moved to Rio de Janeiro to begin our work, we moved into a mission station which was the largest in the world. There were so many MKs going to the American school across town that it was necessary to charter a bus. The number had since dwindled, but the age gap was still there. The MK closest to Ryan's age of four was sixteen years old.

One might ask, "But what about the MK's peer group among the nationals? Surely there are boys and girls their age where you live."

Though this may be true, it still may take on quite a different dynamic than what you might expect. For example, an MK from Indonesia offers these insights.

To an Indonesian an average American is considered rich. This will often bring people either asking for or wanting to borrow some money "to go visit a brother" or "to attend a friend's wedding" or for various other reasons.

Many Indonesians dislike foreigners from any other country. This type is hard to make friends with and to win to Christ. If you think, "Well, why shouldn't they like Americans?" first think how some Americans mistreat other foreigners. Another thing that takes much getting used to is how many of the Indonesian children yell at you. They usually think that you are Dutch. This is because the Netherlands used to govern Indonesia, and they are the only white people many Indonesians know about.

Unless you play with Indonesian boys you usually do not have many friends. Because of this I often miss playing team sports such as football, baseball, and softball. Usually there are only a few missionaries in the same city with you, and I often get tired of playing with and being around the same person all the time.

Three MKs, one from the Philippines and another from Venezuela and a third from Japan, explained this type of isolation from their experiences.

"I had a tendency to draw away from situations I didn't like or understand because I was the only girl my age in the mission and was isolated. When I went to mission meetings, I would dread it and would stay in my parents' room."

The second responded, "I felt the same way." While the third added, "The older girls made fun of me and didn't want me around."

There are some positive aspects that can result from this situation. One aspect would be a great facility in communicating with adults.

An MK from Israel said, "There is greater communication between the generations abroad than in the United States."

An MK from the Philippines offered. "I had little contact with kids my age with similar interests and ideas. My family then had to be my friends. I believe that because of this our family was closer than most families in the US. I believe I got to know my parents and brothers better because we were almost always together (we didn't go to school each day—we studied at home)."

Spiritual Development

Delcie (Mrs. William R.) Wakefield wrote: "Many of the opportunities children normally have in the United States through well-developed programs and activities of churches, schools, and communities are unavailable to most missionary children, except in some of the larger cities."[28]

I might add here that no other country enjoys as well-defined or as well-financed youth ministires as we do in our churches here.

"Most of the churches are young," she continued, "and underdeveloped, with services geared to meet basic needs of young national Christians; consequently, the missionary child's spiritual instruction may be lacking, unless parents find additional ways to meet this need."[29]

Diane Williams, journeyman to the Philippines from 1969-71 and MK teacher, shared these insights about spiritual development. "The missionary family lives, studies, plays, and worships together, and the family unit is a complete way of life for this group of people." Concerning MKs, she went on to say, "These young people have been brought up with a faith in God and mankind that reaches deeper than any ocean and wider than any sea. And because they live with their faith every day, this aspect of life helps them through any crisis."[30]

Living in a foreign country with the opportunity to observe firsthand many different religions has the potential of helping the MK deepen his or her own religious convictions.

An MK from Indonesia explains it in this manner:

"You are able to see a larger variety of religions. You are able to observe how they worship, what they worship, where they worship, when or what day, time, etc. they worship and many other parts of the religion in a way [that] is helpful."

Several MKs say their circumstances contributed to real spiritual growth, strengthened by seeing God act in difficult settings, and nurtured by "aunts and uncles" (other missionaries) who loved them as their own.[31]

"That's where I started to see the Christian life was more than going to church," said Janene Weller, MK from Singapore. "I feel fortunate to have been brought up under really godly men and women."[32]

Alan Robson, MK from Liberia, enthusiastically expressed it: "My family life overseas was great. I grew very fast in my spiritual life."

Certainly, the faith of their parents becomes a model in the MK's spiritual development. Franklin Fowler reflected upon this aspect as he wrote:

"My parents' dedication has continually been an inspiration; their faith has sustained me through the years."[33]

What better heritage could parents leave a child?

Mission Family

All families enjoy their privacy, just as do individuals. In some missionary families, this will take on a new meaning. Albert McClellan expressed:

Joining a mission is like joining a patriarchal family where the family itself is the patriarch. Even though the Foreign Mission Board very carefully instructs new missionaries on the uniqueness of the mission group experience, they are never really quite prepared for it. The mission finally decides where you are to work, where you are to live, what kind of car you will drive. In large measure it determines the education of your children and the time of your furlough. Then in some cases it votes to invite you back again or not to invite, depending on your performance and your relationships.[34]

This may require a real adjustment in many families.

The Cultural Model of the Family

Family life in the foreign country makes its impact upon the family life of the missionary. Naturally, the more positive the model, the more likely that its effect will be positive upon the missionary family.

Many cultures demonstrate the very high level of unity among family members, for example, Latin American and Oriental families.

Over and over again MKs commented to me verbally or in writing about the closeness of the family in their given culture.

An MK from Spain was typical of many when he shared a very positive attitude about his family and then concluded, "My attitude is probably a result of the Spanish culture, that is, model of the family."

Education in the home

We will look at this more in depth later in this chapter, but I have included it here because it is a very real adjustment that many missionary families face. Delcie Wakefield shares this concern in this observation:

Many mothers teach their children from kindergarten through grade eight. When they have several children, this can be a full-time job that consumes most of the day in preparation and teaching. Most of the women are not trained as school teachers, and often there is no other child with whom to compare her child. Thus, she always carries the concern and anxiety of trying to determine if her child is receiving an adequate education; being objective is never easy in making this evaluation.[35]

Pat (Mrs. James C., Jr.) Muse in Ecuador addresses the special benefits of this responsibility as she wrote, "I know of no other relationship quite like the one of being both mother and schoolteacher to my own children."[36]

Different Demands on Time

Just as the concept of the family can vary from culture to culture, so can the concept of time. This requires an adjustment by the missionary. Basically, you could divide the time demands into three areas.

1. Fewer distractions—missionary homes do not have the influence of television that is apparent in the US.

An MK from Indonesia commented: "There is no 'idiot box' sitting in your living room (at least not in ours) which you spend hours watching, and even if there is one you do not watch it as much as you would in the states."

MK Joy Hill of Nigeria agreed and reflected, "There's not such developed television, radio, and other entertainment to take away from time spent together."

2. The likelihood of more quality time for the family— Mareida Grossman, MK to Senegal, stated, "We were a lot closer and always played games and sang together as a family. We were much more intimate with each other than we would have been in the US, I know."

An MK from Nigeria added, "We spend more time together on the field because there is less to do. You feel the need to have family support because you are in another country."

An MK from Mexico affirmed this feeling as she shared, "Family life overseas was more simple and closely knit. Life here [in the US] is more rushed and full of worry."

Andrew Bergquist, MK from Taiwan, related: "Overseas the family is the center of life because there are few nighttime activities to get you involved other than your family [activities]."

Rilda J. Smith, MK from Tanzania, summed it up from her personal experience:

"As a family overseas we were together and would play games, sit and talk, etc. in the evenings. Here in the US I have noticed that everyone is always running here and there, and the family is never together to talk and share. I feel it is vital to the growth of each member to talk things out together."

3. A greater emphasis on the immediate family— Thomas Hogue, MK from Taiwan, stated: "Since we were away from other relatives, much emphasis was put on the immediate family."

Special holidays such as Christmas and Thanksgiving, normally spent with parents of the missionaries and grandparents of the MKs, are celebrated by the immediate family or several missionary families together.

Trips to see relatives are not possible. All of this contributes to more time for the family to spend together.

Development of Adequate Social and Recreational Activities

This would be desired by every parent for their child, but it may take on a significant challenge within the missionary family overseas.

The concept of a neighborhood as we have in the US may be nonexistent in another country where living space is crowded and houses have nonexistent yards. Being Americans may mean that you cannot turn your children loose to play without direct supervision as you might in the US. The responsibility for finding satisfactory substitutes lies with the parents.

Rebekah Emmanuel, MK from Japan, described:

"I can talk to any other MK and understand him. Tanzania—I've never been there, but so what? Richard [Richard Knapp, MK from Tanzania] and I have gone through similar experiences. There is just a union among all the MKs here."[37]

Not only does being part of the missionary family overseas bring you a closer identification with other MKs sharing the same experiences, it often entitles MKs to witness firsthand world events that one only reads about in the newspaper or sees on the nightly news in the US.

Missionaries Emmett and LaNell Barnes, along with their three sons, Randal (age 12), Steve (age 4), and Mark (age 2) arrived in Lebanon in 1967 in the wake of the Six Day War.

According to LaNell, world events are more than newspaper items.

Back in 1978 there was a week or so when the boys just couldn't go to school. . . . We had gotten their homework and their books and had assignments to do at home.

One day I was checking to see if Steven was doing his history. He had set up a little table outside, which was probably a mistake. There was a bombardment going on in Beirut. I said, "Steven, are you doing your history?"

"Mom," he said, "I am not doing it; I am watching history being made!"[38]

The Educational Process of MKs

As MKs settle into their homes in other countries, they and their parents will face the prospect of education. How and where will they receive it? And will it be adequate?

There are basically four options that exist educationally for MKs. First, education in the home; second, education at the national school level (use of the public or private system attended by the nationals); third, education at an

American or European-type school; fourth, education through boarding school.

About 90 percent of the children of overseas Southern Baptist missionaries go to college.

Currently, 561 MKs are enrolled in colleges and universities in the United States and overseas institutions.[39]

It has been said that possibly more tears have been shed by parents and children regarding schooling than over any other part of missionary life[40]—especially when separation is involved.

"This is the only thing I face which I might call a *sacrifice*," said one missionary mother.[41]

In the past consultants to the Board have suggested that sending a child to a boarding school or his enrollment in a local or nearby American school would minimize educational problems. Of course, not every parent would agree with this from their personal experience.[42]

Fowler feels that "much emphasis—perhaps too much —has been placed on quality education for the missionary child. 'Preparing him for college' sometimes has taken on undue proportions. Too often it has become the only priority."[43]

I tend to agree. Regardless of which method of education is chosen, you will find positive and negative factors for each option.

Before looking at the four options, let me draw four conclusions about MK education.

Four Conclusions Concerning MK Education

1. The overwhelming majority of missionaries are satisfied with the education their children received.

I asked the missionaries of the South Brazil mission this question (bearing in mind that this would include supplemental home education, boarding school, attendance and graduation from a national school or an American school or combination of the two): "Are you satisfied with the quality of education received by your child overseas?" Eighty-three percent responded yes; 10 percent responded no; and 7 percent were unsure.

On a much broader scale I sent surveys to mission stations around the world. Missionaries representing fifty-five different countries responded. I asked for a response to the statement: "As a result of the educational method used with my child/children, I feel they are as well educated as their peers in the US."

The response once again, regardless of the method of education, was overwhelmingly positive. Ninety-six percent felt that their child was as well educated as their peers in the US. Three percent were unsure while only one percent responded negatively.

I feel it is noteworthy to mention that within the positive responses 13 percent of them observed that their child's education was not just equal to that of their peers but superior.

2. The MKs themselves feel that their educational background prepared them well for college. You must bear in mind that these MKs are already enrolled in college with anywhere from nearly one semester of college units completed to several years.

Many advantages were listed by the MKs, including contact with teachers who would work with you on a one-to-one basis due to a small class; the teaching abilities of American teachers overseas were felt to be superior to those stateside; very strict academic discipline was noted; a broad variety of courses was offered; an ability to solve problems on their own (since there was not always the luxury of a teacher to explain them) was learned; correspondence courses were felt to be well designed academically; and excellent field trips were considered a plus as was the learning of the national language.

3. The result is academic success, in many cases greater
than would have been possible had their education been
in the United States.

Winston Crawley affirms this:

Regardless of the type of school, . . . "the arrangements made
for the schooling of the children of missionaries almost always
put them academically ahead of what they would have
achieved had they been in the usual American schools," although, he added, "there may be a few exceptional school systems in the US where this would not apply."[44]

Truman S. Smith maintains that "Academically we find
children of missionaries achieving on the level of the children of vocational religious workers here in the states."[45]
While Susi Lockard pointed out, "The records, it should
be noted, indicate that children taught at home for the
first three or four years usually become better than average students in high school and college, gaining excellent
foundations in math and English and in self-discipline
about school work."[46]

4. The majority do not feel that their method of education cost them overall in their ability to relate to their
peers in college.

In the Lane survey, the question was asked: "Do you
feel being an MK has inhibited you socially among your
peer group in college?" Eighty-two percent said no, 13
percent said yes while 5 percent responded that they
were "unsure."[47]

An MK from Chile expressed the thought well when he
said, "I think most of the 'real' problems that we have as
MKs are not real at all, but just a part of the individual
makeup of each person blown up by the fact that MKs are
supposed to have problems."[48]

To be certain, there are adjustments to be made by the
MKs who have spent the majority of their lives in another

culture, and the majority of the MKs handle and resolve these differences very well, but to try to place the "blame" for adjustment difficulties solely upon the educational process would be most unfair.

Four Options for MK Education

Home Education

Teaching children at home is something that many missionaries undertake. It may be that their home is in a remote area where satisfactory schooling does not exist. It may be decided that it is preferable to sending the children off to boarding school. Whatever the reasons, it "presents its own capacity to delight and dishearten. The pleasures outweigh the discouragements, according to several missionary mothers."[49]

The Board is fully aware of the fact that missionary mothers will be faced with this responsibility, so the women receive special instruction in this area while in orientation.[50]

The Board makes available at no cost to the missionary the Calvert Home Instruction Courses to assist the mother in teaching the children. These courses take the child from grade one through grade eight.

Calvert School, Inc., is based in Baltimore and is approved by the Maryland Department of Education. Classrooms of the Calvert Day School serve as experimental laboratories for the Home Instruction Courses and influence their periodic updating.[51]

The Advisory Teaching Service includes evaluation of lessons by a Calvert teacher, airmail return of lessons to the pupil, issue of a certificate of completion for courses and provision of a transcript when the child enters a US school.[52]

Beyond grade eight, correspondence courses are offered by the University of Nebraska (206 different courses during a recent school year). These courses are prepared by certified secondary teachers and are accredited by the state of Nebraska which also authorized the university to grant diplomas.[53]

Costs are calculated on a course-to-course basis.[54] A counselor advises students about courses and graduation requirements. The course credits are generally accepted for admission to US universities and colleges.[55]

All costs for the courses are at Board expense. If the missionary mother feels it necessary to ask for assistance in teaching her children, the "Manual for Missionaries" contains this statement of policy: "In cases involving three or more children, a tutor may be employed or a journeyman or Mission Service Corps or extended-term volunteer requested to help with the teaching. In cases where fewer than three children are involved, the justification of the teaching assignment depends upon another valid half-time assignment."[56] In other words, the teaching would be considered half of the assignment and other responsibilities would need to make up the second half of the total assignment.

Missionary Shirley (Mrs. L. Steve) Ditmore of Peru shared her experience with a journeyman.

> Because the children and I had too much "togetherness," we asked the mission to seek a missionary journeyman. Linda Smith, a young college graduate, arrived in Piura in August 1968 to begin her two-year journeyman term. Truly an answer to prayer, she taught Susan the fourth and fifth grades and Steve the sixth and seventh.[57]

Journeymen are provided with special assistance and training as they go to teach MKs. They will know of existing special needs (in their pupils and teaching materials), availability of common items on the field, and will be aware of special reading materials that may be needed, all prior to their departure.[58]

Journeymen will teach in English, use the pledge to the US flag, a patriotic song, and discuss current North American events on a weekly basis while maintaining a balance with the local customs and culture.[59]

Ask an MK who studied by correspondence to relate his feelings about it. Chances are, you'll receive mixed reactions.

Doug Brock, MK from the Philippines, shared:

"I studied two years of elementary school and high school by correspondence. I learned much more than most kids in public schools. I also learned good study habits."

An MK from North Brazil had the opposite experience. She shared:

"I studied by correspondence courses a big part of my life. I didn't like it very much. I felt when I came to the states on furloughs that I didn't quite know how to react in a classroom situation."

Concerning his study program by correspondence, another MK from Indonesia commented, "There is no competition."

The lack of competition and social contact are drawbacks plus the added responsibility placed upon the mother as teacher unless she can secure a journeyman or share the responsibilities with other mothers.

Yet, as in other challenges we have examined, the same still holds true. The potential exists to make it a very positive experience, deepening the relationship between parent and child.

As Marsha (Mrs. Mike) Key of Togo put it, "Teaching my own children consumes most of my time and energy. At first, I was resentful that I didn't have much time left over for 'mishing' (being a missionary). I've come to understand the importance and responsibility of educating the children. Even if I teach them through high school, our years together are numbered," and overall she concluded, "I believe the frustration is at a minimum and fulfillment is definitely reaching up toward the maximum."[60]

Education at the National School Level

Many MKs attend the national schools in the country where they are serving. The Board encourages missionary parents in this direction. The missionary manual states, "In places where quality education is offered by free national schools, missionary parents working with nationals are encouraged to send their children to the national schools."[61]

Truman Smith adds, "Many of the schools that they attend overseas are excellent academically. Some of them may be limited in some subject areas, particularly the sciences, if they are in a very small school without much laboratory equipment. However, I have not discovered this to be generally a handicap that lingers."[62]

Ellen Sue (Mrs. Phil) Overton of Barbados, West Indies, and Lamar Tribble of Bolivia are typical of missionaries who sent their children to public schools and indicated that they felt the education experience was equal to that obtained in the US.

Ellen Sue responded, "All the kids have gone to public schools when of a good quality." Added Lamar, "They [all three Tribbles] attended our Baptist High School in Temuco, Chile, which is open to any Chilean child. They were not separated with only North Americans but rather enjoyed their educational years with the Chileans."

One MK from Brazil commented on a negative aspect when he stated, "My school was really small, and I did not have to study very much. The school was *not* strict, so I did what I wanted; now my study habits are the 'pits' and I'm having trouble."

Jim Crawford, MK from Venezuala, saw his experience in positive terms and related, "The school I attended in Venezuela is superior to the schools here in the states. I was completely ready to enter college."

MKs attending either the national public school systems or national Baptist schools may supplement their study by making use of American history or English correspondence courses.[63]

Some MKs, like Karen Doyle of Guatemala, will have several forms of education. She reflected on this experience.

"I was taught by correspondence course in grades 1-6. I also attended national school in the same grades. I was in American school [220 students] from grades 7-10. I feel well prepared for my college experience and see no disadvantages to having gone to school overseas."

Winston Crawley noted a major consideration in whether or not to use the national school:

The national public school systems are not necessarily bypassed in educational processes of the missionary child. Most of these schools, however, are already overcrowded and cannot accommodate children from the American community. Language differences create an additional barrier to their utilization.[64]

Education in an American or European-Type School

Concerning this option, missionaries receive this orientation: "In places where an adequate education is offered in both American schools and other English language schools, the less expensive should be chosen."[65]

The MK may choose from schools located on US military installations, such as Clark Air Force Base in the

Philippines. These schools are open on a space-available basis, and tuition must be paid by nonmilitary families. Where this is a viable option, the Board pays the expenses.

A second possibility for the American community is American-sponsored schools supported by the office of overseas schools of the US Department of State. In 1965-66 there were 121 of these schools in 75 countries, with an enrollment of 25,082 American children and 21,045 other children from 96 countries.[66]

Enrollment in these State Department Schools ranges from less than a dozen students in remote areas to thousands in population centers. The institutions exist both to fulfill educational needs of the American community and to express the philosophy and methods of American education to the host country.[67]

MKs and parents alike generally rate American schools overseas quite high in terms of academic preparation for college.

Typical of such comments are:

It was a college-prep school. Its advantages were that it was not an American school but an international one, thus we learned of other cultures from our classmates. It prepared me for a college work load—developed my study habits well.—MK Edie Walker, South Brazil.

We attended an American school, but I noticed that it is a lot harder than schooling in the states.—MK Miriam Nicholson, Liberia.

I went to an American school, and it prepared me very well for my college experience. Most of my courses seem easy.—MK Jeff Bailey, Argentina.

MKs may attend British schools. Those who did so seemed quite satisfied as the comments from MKs in Zimbabwe, India, and Hong Kong will illustrate:

I was educated under the British system which gave me a

very good preparation for college. It was strict and hard work, and I missed out on a lot of fun in American high schools, which I do regret, but I'd never change my past if I could.—MK Brigitte Atnip.

[I attended] mostly British systems in earlier years and American school in high school. It was a good chance to experience both. British [school] is too academic, and American is too much on the extracurricular activities. I tried to find a good balance between the two.—MK Steve Baker.

High standards were set in British government schools with good moral discipline.—MK Joseph Hollis.

Still other possibilities exist educationally.

MKs in Chile may take advantage of a German-run school, and those MKs in Japan may take advantage of a school run according to the Canadian system.

These schools, including the British schools, are known as third country schools—since they are neither American nor national, but exist in the host country to serve another foreign group.[68]

Education Through a Boarding School

This type of education is difficult in the experience of both the parents and child.

A missionary mother commented:

A missionary family faces a difficult time when a child has to go away to a boarding high school. Often this means that the teenager can return home only once or twice a year. The idea of having someone else care for your children during these formative years can cause anxiety on the part of the missionary parents.[69]

The Foreign Mission Board has a definite policy concerning the necessity of using a boarding school. Some elements in the policy are:

1. All travel expenses are paid for two round trips per

year from the place of residence to the boarding school (the trip to school at the beginning of the year and the return trip at the end count as one trip). A third round trip is authorized when a bona fide holiday period lasts at least four full days.

2. All tuition fees are at Board expense (not including music, art, and fees for food).

3. Travel expense can be provided for one parent to visit the child at his school location once during each academic year, when missionary children attend school in a country near that of the parent's assignment (not including the US).[70]

It is possible, under certain circumstances, for parents to send their children to the United States to attend high school.

While one might jump to the conclusion that boarding schools pose all kinds of problems for MKs and their parents, you might be surprised to see how positive many MKs are toward the experience. Of course, you must also bear in mind that all boarding schools are not alike; therefore, the experiences of various MKs will be different.

Consider these comments:

I lived in a dorm my last two years of school. The community was very protected. Many problems I have already faced, I never came into contact with at boarding school.

And the opposite experience;

I personally see no disadvantages of my type of schooling which was at a boarding school for MKs in another country and a good 1,500 miles from my parents. It taught me to be on my own, to be able to make my own decisions, and to appreciate my parents. I grew up there with MKs from other denominations and learned a lot from them and was really able to see what and why I believed as I do. I think boarding school is the greatest!—MK from Tanzania.

Consider the decision of Jonnie Hill, an MK from Liberia, who decided to leave home and live in an MK home.

An MK's Search for Home

"In the beginning was the Word, and the Word was with God, and the Word was God." It was this Word that helped me to make a difficult decision and resolve a resulting conflict.

Over a year ago I made the decision to leave my parents and live at the MK home in Monrovia for the second semester of my eighth year in school. It was a decision my parents wanted me to make.

There were several methods I used in making my decision. First, I tried procrastination, waiting to see if Mom and Dad would make it for me. When that didn't work, I opened my Bible expecting my eyes to just land on a yes or no. That didn't work. Then, like Gideon, I asked for signs.

When I moved to the MK home six months later, there began a new conflict in my mind. Where was home? I wasn't sure. I lived in two different houses at the time. I had lived in five different cities and two countries. So I defined "home" in my own way. I began to call both houses "home" because in both "homes" there were people I share with. In one home I live with those of my own flesh and blood. In the other home I live with those whom I have adopted as my family. Both homes have the key ingredient—love. Yet I still have another home—heaven. There I have an even larger family, all of us sisters and brothers in Christ saved by his blood.

Every year I have two homes I live in: one home where I go to school, the other where I stay during vacation. Along life's walk I'll have other homes. The greatest home will be that in heaven, the home where the Word first began.—Jonnie Hill.[71]

We would do well to prayerfully remember missionary families who face this separation, their sons and daughters who leave home to attend these schools, those who have the great responsibility of being substitute mothers and fathers to these MKs away from their homes, and those who teach them.

Having considered the MK's family overseas, its dynamics and challenges, and the MK's education, let's examine the appointment process: how it all begins and how the children are involved in each step. The problem of mobility will be examined, and you will see why being an MK can be such a positive experience.

Notes

1. Susan S. Longest, "I Am an MK," *Foreign Missionary Intercom*, Jan. 1982, p. 3.

2. Kathy Steele, "Naming Some Stresses," *The Commission*, Dec. 1981, p. 9.

3. Martha Skelton, "Missionary Families: Some Stresses and Strengths," *The Commission*, Dec. 1981, p. 8.

4. Ibid., p. 11.

5. Arthur W. Combs and Donald Snygg, *Individual Behavior* (New York: Harper and Row, 1959), pp. 85-86.

6. Sidney L. Workman, "Hazards of Rearing Children in Foreign Countries," *American Journal of Psychiatry* 128:8, Feb. 1972, p. 107.

7. Mary Ann Ward, "MK Letters," *Accent* 10, July 1975, p. 27.

8. Franklin T. Fowler, "The Third World Culture of the MK," *The Commission* 33, Dec. 1970, p. 3.

9. William C. Viser, "A Psychological Profile of Missionary Children in College and the Relationship of Intense Group Therapy to Weekly Group Therapy in the Treatment of Personality Problems as Reflected by the Minnesota Multiphasic Personality Inventory," Ed.D. dissertation, Southwestern Baptist Theological Seminary (1978), pp. 113-114.

10. Leland Webb and Dora Kelly, "Finding Her Role," *The Commission*, Nov. 1974, p. 5.

11. Ibid.

12. Susi Lockard, "Partners in Preparation," *The Commission*, Feb. 1978, p. 7.

13. Delcie Wakefield, "The Versatile 'Homemaker,'" *The Commission*, Nov. 1974, p. 8.

14. Charles H. Howell, "Family Shock," *The Commission*, Nov. 1974. p. 8.

15. Lockard, "Partners in Preparation," p. 7.

16. Webb and Kelly, "Finding Her Role," p. 5.

17. Ibid.

18. Ibid.

19. Ibid.

20. H. Victor Davis to William C. Viser, Oct. 1, 1981.

21. Lockard, "Partners in Preparation," p. 3.

22. Interview with H. Victor Davis, Feb. 21, 1983.

23. Laura S. Lane, "Missionary Kids Share Their Feelings About Being MKs," mimeographed, Carson-Newman College, Jefferson City, Tennessee, 1976, p. 5.

24. William C. Viser, "Survey Concerning MKs," South Brazil Mission Meeting, Serra Negra, Brazil, 1979.

25. William C. Viser, "MK Weekend Survey," MK Weekend, Richmond, Virginia, 22-25 Nov. 1979.

26. Norman Jameson, " 'Missionary Kids' Feel God Calling Home," *Baptist Standard*, April 13, 1983, p. 20.

27. Albert McClellan, "The Anguishes of the Missionary," *The Baptist Program*, Oct. 1977, p. 6.

28. Wakefield, "The Versatile Homemaker," p. 9.

29. Ibid., p. 5.

30. Diane Williams, "A Bridge for the Cultural Gap," *The Commission*, Aug. 1971, p. 24.

31. Norman Jameson, " 'Missionary Kids' Feel God Calling Home," *Baptist Standard*, Apr. 13, 1983, p. 13.

32. Ibid.

33. Fowler, "The Third World Culture," p. 3.

34. McClellan, "The Anguishes of the Missionary," p. 6.

35. Wakefield, "The Versatile Homemaker," p. 9.

36. Webb and Kelly, "Finding Her Role," p. 5.

37. Teresa Shields, "They Share a Common Heritage," *The Commission*, Mar. 1976, p. 26.

38. Martha Skelton, " 'Mom, I'm Watching History,' MK Says," *The Commission*, Dec. 1981, p. 13.

39. The Foreign Mission Board of the Southern Baptist Convention, "Margaret Fund Students, February 5, 1986."

40. Marina Menzies, "Top Ten Prayer Needs," *The Commission,*Dec. 1981, p. 29.

41. Wakefield, "The Versatile Homemaker," pp. 9-10.

42. Richmond *News Leader*, Nov. 28, 1970, p. 3.

43. Fowler, "The Third World Culture," p. 3.

44. Susan S. Cohen, "Classrooms: A Wide Variety," *The Commission*, Aug. 1971, p. 9.

45. Truman S. Smith to Tina Block Ediger, May 1, 1979.

46. Lockard, "Partners in Preparation," pp. 1-3.

47. Lane, "Missionary Kids Share Their Feelings About Being MKs," p. 4.

48. Ibid.

49. Skelton, "Missionary Families: Some Stresses and Strengths," p. 8.

50. Lockard, "Partners in Preparation," p. 1.

51. Cohen, "Classrooms, A Wide Variety," p. 8.

52. Cohen, "Classrooms, A Wide Variety," p. 8.

53. Ibid.

54. Mary Reid to William C. Viser.

55. Cohen, "Classrooms, a Wide Variety," p. 8.

56. Office of Overseas Operations, "Manual for Missionaries," Foreign Mission Board Southern Baptist Convention, United States of America, Richmond, Virginia, n.d.: Section Number 2000, p. 411.

57. Shirley Ditmore, "School on the Roof," *The Commission*, Aug. 1971, p. 11.

58. Foreign Mission Board of the Southern Baptist Convention, "Education of MKs," mimeographed, Orientation and Development Department, n.d., p. 1.

59. Ibid., p. 2.

60. Skelton, "Missionary Families: Some Stresses and Strengths," p. 8.

61. "Manual for Missionaries," 2000:411, p. 2 of 3.

62. Smith to Ediger.

63. Cohen, "Classrooms, A Wide Variety," p. 9.

64. Ibid.

65. "Manual for Missionaries," p. 8.

66. Cohen, "Classrooms, a Wide Variety," pp. 7-8.

67. Ibid., p. 8.

68. Ibid., p. 9.

69. Nancy Blevins Ryals, "Missionary Families," *Royal Service*, Jan. 1977, p. 21.

70. "Manual for Missionaries," p. 8.

71. Jonnie Hill, "An MK's Search for Home," *Foreign Missionary Intercom*, Nov. 1981, p. 2.

Beginnings

Then Jesus came to them and said, "All authority in heaven and on earth has been given to me. Therefore go and make disciples of all nations, baptizing them in the name of the Father and of the Son and of the Holy Spirit, and teaching them to obey everything I have commanded you. And surely I will be with you always, to the very end of the age" (Matt. 28:18-20, NIV).

What not to say to MKs prior to departure from the United States to their country of service:

"You don't want to leave here, do you?"

New appointee Judy Garrett related that their children were thrilled about moving until they were frequently reminded that going to the field meant leaving their home. What they needed was positive support from adults—not doubt casting.

MK Abigail Smith of Indonesia wrote:

"Our leaving the States is hard on most of us. I mean in things like leaving your relatives. When you leave, it always seems to be a last good-bye, because you never know what will happen. Another is having to leave all your friends whom you have known for such a long time."

2

Beginnings:
From Contacts to
Contracts

Have you ever wondered what it might be like to live overseas as a foreign missionary and raise a family? You have heard countless numbers of missionaries speak of it. You have seen them with their families standing before you. The reports they have given have moved you and inspired you to feel deeply for them.

Put yourself in their place for a moment. What would it be like? How would you begin as a foreign missionary? Where would you start, and what process would you go through? Of course, on the heels of such thinking would always come the question, "And what about my children?"

Let's start at the very beginning of your process.

The Foreign Mission Board of the Southern Baptist Convention, like other denominational mission boards, both makes and receives contacts in many different ways.

You might want to know more about missions, possibly feeling that God is leading you into this area. You would contact the FMB (Foreign Mission Board) through the personnel department requestion information.

You could respond to an invitation during a worship service, camp or retreat, revival, or a message given by a missionary. Your name could be sent to the FMB as one having expressed such an interest. The Board would, in turn, contact you.

On a month-to-month basis, the Foreign Mission Board receives approximately ninety contacts per month.[1] In a recent year initial contacts totaled 1,078.[2] Many of these contacts will be from couples with infants or young children. Of all couples appointed in that same year, 79.4 percent had children—the average age being 5.4 years.[3]

As you consider missions, you would likely ask questions such as:

1. Where do the children fit into the appointment process?

2. Is consideration given to their emotional needs and how living overseas will affect them?

3. How does the Board take into account the country where the family may be appointed and the child?

4. Exactly what areas concern the Board in regard to these future MKs?

You might even be surprised to discover that children can stop the appointment process temporarily or permanently.

You will learn the answers to all of these plus many more questions in this chapter.

Imagine that you have in hand the brochure made available by the Board entitled simply "The Appointment Process."[4] Ten steps are listed and briefly explained. Let's examine them in the light of the children.

The Appointment Process

1. Initial contact is made with the Foreign Mission Board indicating interest in overseas mission work. As you would expect in this step, both mother and father consider the implications of what a move like this will mean to their son or daughter today or their child yet unborn.

As I look back on our thinking at this time, I remember that we were settled in a comfortable home with a yard in front and a fenced in backyard suitable for a growing

boy to romp and play, a challenging position on a prominent church staff, and an ever-widening circle of personal
friends for Susan and me as well as Ryan. We wondered
what would a sudden change in environment do to Ryan,
or to us. Could he or would he make the transition without
it being overly difficult? How flexible would he be? What
would this move mean in terms of his spiritual, physical,
emotional, and social development?

We certainly were no different from other parents at
this point, and, like others, we talked with other missionaries and personal friends. We sounded out parents and
family, talked it over between ourselves and with Ryan,
and, above all, we prayed and prayed.

I believe all parents do many, if not all, of the same
things we did. Children figure prominently in the minds
of their mother and father and are an important part of
this initial contact.

As the contact is made with the Board, it is then chan-
neled to the Department of Personnel Selections where
one of five people will respond to the contact. Each of
these five is known as a "candidate consultant" and has
the responsibility of one section of the country. These five
sections, each with a certain number of units, are (1) The
Atlantic Coast Region, (2) The North Central Region, (3)
The South Central Texas Region, (4) The North Central
Texas Region, and (5) The Western Region. What is a unit?
A *unit* is a shortened term for a family or single appointee.
For example, in 1981 the number of units within section
one—the Atlantic Coast Region—including Southeastern
Baptist Theological Seminary totaled 230. That means
that this section includes either 230 families and/or sin-
gles.

In 1981 the North Central Region—including Southern
Baptist Theological Seminary—totaled 241 units. The
South Central Region—including New Orleans Theologi-

cal Seminary—totaled 270 units while the North Central Texas Region including Southwestern Baptist Theological Seminary totaled 362 units. The Western Region—including both Midwestern and Golden Gate Baptist Theological Seminaries totaled 311.[5]

2. Candidate consultant shares information concerning current needs and qualifications through letters, phone conversations, and mission information conferences.

In a recent interview, program manager William A. Krushwitz shared three typical questions asked by couples in these contacts. Of the three, the third was, "What about raising a family overseas?"[6]

It would be difficult to find a couple who did not have some basis for which to ask a question such as the one above. Some would base their questions on what they have heard missionary speakers relate while on furlough or former friendships with MKs in college. Still other information could come from mission studies or from books on missions. Occasionally, a person might develop concepts or form opinions on life overseas based on incorrect information. I want to examine this in greater detail later in this book.

Beyond a doubt, children do play a prominent role from the very beginning of the appointment process both in the hearts and minds of their parents and to the Foreign Mission Board as well. You might say that it is at this point that children enter officially into the picture.

3. Inquirer shares basic credentials on information form; medical history is shared through a preliminary health questionnaire at the appropriate time.

The basic health of each child is an important part of the appointment process, for a couple will only be as successful in their work as the family is basically healthy.

When Susan and I were going through the appointment procedure, we filled out the necessary medical forms for both of us and for our then two-year-old son, Ryan. In addition to the necessity of our undergoing medical examinations, Ryan also received a thorough physical; personal history about his birth was discussed; pulse, blood pressure, weight, and height, and tests such as blood, urine, tuberculosis, and serology were all taken. Recommendations by the examining physician were requested. After his examination, the physician filled out and mailed his report to the office of the medical consultant directed by Franklin T. Fowler.

In this office reports are studied and approved or, perhaps, not approved. On the average, 20 percent of the applications are not approved for medical reasons.[7]

It is not only the physical side of the child which receives the interest of the Foreign Mission Board but also the emotional state.

Preliminary health questionnaires seek information from parents regarding possible emotional problems with their children. Medical forms to be filled out by examining physicians are concerned with this area as well. For example, the following questions are among those the physician responds to:

(1) Do you recommend examinee (child) from the point of view of physical fitness and emotional stability to live in a foreign country with missionary parents? Any reservations?

(2) Comments as to possible behavioral problems?

(3) Comments as to possible developmental problems?

(4) Comments as to possible psychiatric problems?[8]

From the standpoint of the Board, the emotional state of the child is not only considered from the doctor's perspective but also from the personal involvement of the Board.

Don A. Reavis, candidate consultant to the Board, echoed this concern and involvement as he shared with me:

"It is valid to say that children are one concern throughout the entire appointment process. It is also a concern as
we work with people who have no children."[9]

During this step of the appointment process, frequent
contact is maintained by the Board with the prospective
couples and vice versa. When it is felt to be helpful, a visit
in the home is arranged. Here, perhaps for the first time,
a contact is made with all members of the family. The staff
member has the opportunity to meet and talk with each
child in the family.

Relating his thoughts about this visit, Don said, "I am
concerned about the general adjustment of the entire
family, including the children. I am watching for social
skills, learning ability, and maturity levels. If a child is not
appropriately mature for his age and sex, this would raise
a rather serious caution flag. Where learning difficulties
are ascertained prior to appointment, a couple may be
delayed until the child is out of the home. It is also of
interest to our staff to note how parents share decision
making with the children."[10]

If it is felt to be necessary, the Board will recommend
that the child have an interview with a psychiatrist who
will be designated by the FMB.

Dr. Henry Holland of Richmond, Virginia, is one psychiatrist whom the Foreign Mission Board often uses. He
recently stated that such an interview (with a child of less
than twelve years of age) would be in order whenever
there is any past history of problems, behavior problems,
or a problem that really exists between the parents which
results in the child becoming the symptomatic individual.
(As a matter of policy, the Foreign Mission Board does not
send the children of prospective missionary parents to a
psychiatrist unless indicated.)

Based upon the results of that interview, the professional opinion of the psychiatrist, and the personnel depart-

ment, the application process may come to a temporary stop or may stop completely.

When a couple with adolescents beyond twelve years of age makes inquiries concerning appointment, a different situation exists.

From his nine years of work with the Board, Dr. Holland commented on this area:

"I believe that the Foreign Mission Baord has found that more problems exist for adolescents going to the mission field than any other group. Adolescence is a difficult period in the stages of development in any family constellation or culture. Peer group involvement and peer group identity during adolescence is extremely important and to translocate adolescents from one culture to another during this period of development is naturally quite stressful."[11]

Don Reavis explained this concern further:

"A lay couple with a twelve-year-old will need to make a move to seminary for twenty hours of theology, to orientation for twelve weeks, to language school for one year to two years of study, and eventually to service on the field. That schedule is difficult at best and would be unusually trying for a teenager."[12]

The actual cutoff time is usually if a child can be through orientation before he or she completes the eighth grade.

According to Don, this allows the child to complete grades nine through twelve prior to returning with the parents during their furlough year. This schedule also allows the parents to be stateside while the child adjusts to college or to a work situation in a stateside setting.[13]

So, as you can see up to this point, the physical *and* emotional health of those to be sent out to other countries all over the world is of great importance and concern to the Foreign Mission Board.

Step number four continues this thread of concern for children on the part of the Foreign Mission Board.

4. Candidates share their pilgrimage through an interpretative historical and life sketch.

This is a confidential and intimate interpretive history of the individual which is approximately ten typewritten pages in length. The husband and wife each compose their own.

The history is required for three reasons:

(1) It enables individuals to better understand themselves and God's leadership in their lives.

(2) It is a help to the personnel secretaries as they attempt to gain a deeper understanding of the candidate.

(3) The psychiatrist is able to make the maximum use of his session with the individual after reading the personal history.

Each personal history is comprised of seven areas.

Early childhood: number of children and ages, conflictual experiences with parents, sibling rivalry, which parent initiated and which implemented family activities, illustrations of the display of affection in the home, experiences of loss or grief and separation or hurt, your happiest childhood experience.

Sexuality: sexual discovery and development, who first gave you instruction—parents or teachers or peers, whether it was adequate, attitude toward sex, sexual needs and how they are fulfilled, marriage (or feelings about it, if single).

Emotional development: family recognition of personal achievements, impressions concerning personal approval or disapproval from family or others, when you left home and readiness for the experience, stressful experiences in the last five years, and how you dealt with them.

Social development: entertainment of relatives and friends in your home during your childhood, early activities outside the home, dating, engagement, recent social activities and community involvements.

Professional identity: what work you do best, recent occupational changes, how you got your present job, professional awards and honors, and areas where further training is desired.

Religious development: early influence, conversion, baptism, church life, call to missions, connection of call with personal training and gifts and capabilities, and recent affirmation of your call by others.

Family relationships: characteristics of children, frequency of contacts with parents and siblings and extended family. As in the other steps of the process, the children enter into the picture by means of the personal history.[14] I can personally testify that thinking through my family relationships and the other six areas was a rewarding and satisfying, though tiring, experience!

5. Qualified candidates receive additional information or feedback from personnel staff at a candidate conference in Richmond. Though the children of the couple do not attend this conference, they become a vital part of the process as the candidates are interviewed concerning their children, family life and other significant aspects, and their preparation to respond to God's call.

6. Candidates undergo medicals, share a statement of belief, and give references from employment and church settings.

Again, the chief concern of the Board for the child is evidenced here, for with every child of five years or older a reference is required from the Sunday School teacher, a school teacher, and a family friend.

These reference forms ask for information in five areas:

(1) How long the information source has known the child and the nature of the relationship.

(2) The sharing of factors from the child's family back-

ground that would affect the child's suitability for missionary life overseas is requested.

(3) The source is also requested to rate the child by checking an already defined category choice as to physical condition, energy level, personal appearance, intelligence, leadership, social acceptability, achievement, emotional stability, attitude, and teamwork.

(4) The source is requested to underscore and illustrate traits, if any, which characterize the child: impotent, sullen, intolerance, argumentative, domineering, and so forth.[15]

7. The candidate's application, sense of calling, and anticipated assignment are reviewed by a committee of Board members. This is all examined carefully, and, of course, pertinent information about the children will be included.

8. The candidates share their sense of leadership with Board members and will be appointed as missionaries. Board members are concerned about the children in many ways. Board member Betty Moore shared with me that, in the interaction which takes place between the Board and the missionary couple, we "inquire of them about how their children are reacting to the prospects of moving and living in another culture. We also inquire about their educational facilities and whether the mother will be required to teach her children."

Betty is typical of Board members who express strong interest in such matters. Her father, S. A. Whitlow, was a well-known Baptist pastor and much beloved in Arkansas and throughout the Convention. Betty moved many times in her childhood, never felt uprooted, and wisely stated, "A good family relationship can prove to be one of the best witnesses a missionary has in the United States or overseas."[16]

9. New missionaries attend "orientation" in preparation

for the move overseas which is step ten. This ninth step is one of the most significant in terms of its effect on the child. It is in preparation for the move to orientation that choices must be made such as:

(1) What belongings of the child or children can we afford to take and what should be given away, thrown away, or sold in a garage sale?

(2) The storage company comes to box up items and carry them to the warehouse to be stored.

(3) The separation and breaking of ties for the move to the Orientation Center—the first of many such to come—is seen and felt by the child.

However, the eight-week session at the Orientation Center held outside of Richmond, Virginia, is an exciting time of transition prior to departure for the assigned field of their parents.

Children continue with their education during the time of orientation. Children from birth to school age (six years) are provided for in day-care facilities staffed by the Mission Board. This enables the parents to participate in orientation sessions during the morning as well as part of the afternoon. It also enables the children to benefit from planned activities and serves as an outlet for their un-bounded energies.

Throughout orientation, the family units eat, study, learn, and play together. Special programs are planned where the children are invited to perform, a children's choir is organized, missions fairs are planned where families take part in representing their various countries, and during the fall period of orientation a Saturday is set aside to provide a time of ministry and fellowship to internationals in the local area. Families are encouraged to keep a notebook on their new country with every family member participating in the project.

These are but a few of the many activities planned to

help families adjust during the transition period and look ahead to their future life in another part of the world.

Evidently, the program as planned succeeds well. Truman Smith shared in an article from *Home Life* entitled "Missionary Families: Human and Heroic."

Recently, in meeting with new missionary families, MKs . . . in grades 3-8 shared some of their thoughts and feelings about moving to another country. Several were excited about learning a new language and experiencing new customs. Most could describe one or more sports or games that they would be learning in their new country. All knew how they would travel and generally the direction they would go, as well as location of their country on a map.

Some of the MKs felt they, too, could tell people about Jesus, especially their new friends. Three mentioned war and guerrilla activity in the countries where they were going. Their concern seemed realistic and yet did not temper their enthusiasm for going.

All had personal belongings including toys that they had not seen in some weeks, and they looked forward to having these items again. In praying together, they mentioned friends who were yet to be made, travel plans that were not yet certain, a family left behind, grandparents they might not see again, looking forward to having their personal items to use again, and for the end of fighting and war.[17]

Enough cannot be said about the importance of communicating to a child what is going on around him and what the future will hold for him.

Edmund Wilson in *The Wound and the Bow* related the case of Rudyard Kipling and how a lack of communication from Kipling's parents severely affected Kipling in the transition that followed.

Rudyard Kipling grew up in India with his parents and native servants until he was six years of age. At this age, his parents decided that he should return to his "home" in England and live with his uncle while completing his education. Unfortunately, his parents never explained why they wanted him to return, and the result was that Kipling became despondent in England and spent hours staring out of one of the windows in his uncle's house. Due to this set of circumstances, he developed partial blindness and a "severe nervous breakdown."

Wilson quoted the sister of Rudyard Kipling:

> I think the real tragedy of our early days [in England] sprang from our inability to understand why our parents had deserted us. We had had no preparation or explanation; it was like a double death, or rather, like an avalanche that had swept away everything happy and familiar . . . . We felt we had been deserted, almost as much as on a doorstep.[18]

Preparation is important and essential for the future adjustment of the MK in his respective country. Concentrated time is spent in doing this while missionary families attend the Missionary Orientation Center.

Preparation also plays a significant role in the return adjustment of MKs as they leave their country to return to the United States in order to begin their college education.

Concerning this aspect of preparation, Dr. William Tanner, while President of Oklahoma Baptist University, wrote an article entitled "Strictly Personal for Parents of MKs." Of the seven suggestions he made as president of a school which annually enrolls numerous MKs, it is not surprising that the suggestion at the top of the list was: "Prepare your child and yourself for the separation."[19]

Roots

It has been well established that our society is a mobile one. This is all the more true for the missionary family and has a substantial affect on the children. Just how substantial depends on several factors.

Richard Rahe, in his book *Feel Younger, Live Longer*, made a list of forty-three events, each one with corresponding value on a scale of impact from the highest to the lowest. He entitled the list "The Stress of Adjusting to Change." He placed moving twenty-eighth on a list or close to the top of the second half of events leading to stress.[20]

How stressful a move or moves are for MKs depends on the ages of the MKs involved, how well they are prepared for the move far in advance of the actual day, how much they understand about the move itself, the degree to which they have been allowed to enter into discussions concerning the move and help make decisions about the move, the feelings of parents and grandparents concerning the move, and, of course, how many moves the MK has already experienced.

Although ours is a mobile society—many of you may have experienced few moves in your lifetime. I never knew but one house for nearly twenty-three years and only two schools before college. I grew up in the same church from Cradle Roll to the College Department. All of my life up to the day I married Susan and our move to Fort Worth was permanency.

When Ryan was born in 1975, we lived in a small three-bedroom home in Fort Worth, Texas. Upon our appointment in July 1978, Ryan, like all MKs, experienced his first of several moves to come. The movers took our furniture and items we had decided to keep and placed them in storage.

Then we packed our car to the absolute maximum plus and set out for the Missionary Orientation Center (MOC) in Callaway Gardens, Georgia, for four months of orientation.

From the few days prior to Christmas—when we left orientation until the day we arrived in Rio de Janeiro, Brazil, we stayed on the road—spending our last few days with family in Tennessee, Arkansas, and Texas—not more than a week in any one place.

On February 1 we arrived in Rio where we spent a few days with missionary colleagues while we received more orientation. Upon arriving in Campinas, the location of our language school, we spent nearly two weeks with another missionary family while we tried to find housing. After finding housing we sunk temporary roots for six months, only to return to the United States for six weeks while we received our permanent visas and naturally spent more time visiting with family in three or four states while awaiting our visas.

We returned to Campinas and our same house where we remained another six months before moving to Rio. At last we finished our schooling and moved to Rio! Since housing was not ready, we stayed with another missionary family for nearly two weeks and finally moved into our first "permanent" home.

This was Ryan's first glimpse of his old toys and belonging in nearly two years. By my own count, Ryan experienced sixteen moves in the two-year period.

Many new missionaries spend a lot of time staying with their missionary colleagues, and moves are the "order of the day" for many also.

It is precisely this aspect of MK life that can be the cause of problems in the future. Franklin Fowler listed it as one of the disadvantages for the MK.[21]

During the preparation of my doctoral thesis I had the privilege of working with thirty-five MKs in small-group sessions. Among the many thoughts expressed were those of frequent mobility and the difficulty of establishing roots.

In one session with a mixed group of MKs representing Argentina, Mexico, Indonesia, Japan, Venezuela, and the Philippines, an MK from Indonesia volunteered that among the factors that make you hesitate to establish roots are your ever-changing environment and the fear of making friendships combined with the hurt following because of their short duration.

Another MK from Venezuela shared that she was constantly moving and the most time spent in one place was five years. She added that when people asked where she was from, she didn't know what to say.

In an article entitled "MK Perspective," Ruth Fowler quoted an MK concerning mobility:

"I don't think you ever get over that. It's really hard when you get settled in a place and then have to say, 'Well, bye. I don't know when I'll see you again.' I think in a way you learn to adapt better, but I think it will always be hard for me."[22] And hard it is for many MKs.

Franklin Fowler feels that the MK soon learns not to let his weight down too much in a new community but rather to develop his own securities within himself and among his siblings and parents. He may at the same time tend not to be too quick to make new friends and thus be somewhat reserved.[23]

Though it can be a difficult situation to deal with, it is not always an impossible one. Depending upon the family structure and the situation, it can have some positive features. The high mobility of the MK should stand him in good stead in the near future. One writer put it in the following manner:

"Alvin Toffler in *Future Shock* thinks the elite of the future will jet from country to country easily adjusting to language and cultural differences. If he is correct, missionary youth are better prepared than most to supply leadership to our world in the future."[24]

One MK summed it up pretty well when she sighed and told me, "I wish that I could have lived a normal life," but, as a big smile spread across her face, "the advantages far outweigh the disadvantages." And so they do.

In two different surveys, the highly positive attitude of MKs toward their MKness was demonstrated.

In 1972, Sophia Gomes, in a paper entitled "Research on Missionary Kids," surveyed forty college-age MKs from twenty different countries. Thirty of the MKs responded. Two particular questions of note were:

"Do you consider it a privilege being an MK?"

"Would you be willing to serve as a foreign missionary if God calls you?"

To the first question, twenty-nine responded positively while one responded negatively. To the second question twenty-seven responded in the positive sense.[25]

Another survey along these lines was taken four years later with a new group of college-age MKs. Laura Sprinkle Lane, daughter of missionaries Dan and Adda Sprinkle in Panama, surveyed fifty MKs with thirty-eight responding.

In response to the question, "Do you consider it a privilege to have been brought up on the foreign mission field?" 97 percent answered yes.[26]

When asked, "Do you feel the positive aspects of being an MK outweigh the negative ones?" 92 percent responded yes.[27]

When questioned as to whether *they* would be willing to raise *their* children on the foreign mission field, 90 percent replied yes.[28]

Mrs. Lane correctly drew the following conclusion, "I think the response to question 16 [the last question above], the fact that 90% of the MKs indicated that they would be willing to raise their own children on the foreign mission field, indicates a highly positive attitude among the group."[29]

She then concluded,

"I sincerely hope that this survey will be of encouragement to young couples interested in going into foreign missions. God takes care of His MKs."[30]

A Positive MK Experience

What are the contributing factors that help make the MK experience such an overwhelmingly positive one from their viewpoint? The following nine are good examples:[31]

1. A greater opportunity for appreciation of what they have in the United States. Mary Ann Ward related that MKs have seen world hunger firsthand. Many have seen poverty, and all are aware that the standard of living enjoyed by most Americans would not be typical in the countries they have called home.[32]

2. A broadening perspective from travel and meeting other people. David Lockard, the former director of Missionary Orientation in Callaway Gardens, Georgia, quotes one MK as saying, "I've become a part of another culture which has broadened my horizons."[33] Another stated, "I have a deeper understanding of people and their needs."[34]

While working on my dissertation, I read a study which compared adolescents from overseas homes (military, federal civilian, missionary, business, and foundation scholar). The missionary student evidenced more components of world-mindedness (the expression or manifestation of open-mindedness toward different concepts of national identity and cross-cultural values) than did any of the other classifications.[35]

3. The opportunity to see mission work firsthand with active participation.[36] One MK expressed by letter how much she missed being a part of her parents' work and

working with laymen from the United States who would come to offer medical care.[37]

4. An appreciation for those who are supporting mission work by offerings and prayers.[38]

5. The opportunity to combine the best of two different cultures.

As a Malaysian MK shared, "The advantages of being an MK greatly outweigh the disadvantages in my mind. While living overseas I'm gaining a knowledge of the rest of the world. I'm learning a culture that is totally different from my American one. I can then pull parts from both of these cultures and put them together. This forms a third culture that is neither American or Malaysian, but both. To me this is really exciting!"[39]

6. Enhanced relationships due to the overseas background. An MK from the Philippines stated, "A lot of people are interested in getting to know you because you've lived overseas." Another offered, "I haven't been as shocked by people different from me."[40]

7. A deeper appreciation for the positive elements of the MK's country as compared to the United States. An MK from Nigeria shared, "The main advantage for me is the unadulterated wildlife and countryside where I grew up."[41]

8. An opportunity to be part of a family at large, an expanded family. Stanley Stamps related that the missionary family fills the void which the grandparents cannot— due to distance and other factors.[42]

9. A deeper knowledge of cultural as well as political occurances. An MK from Japan felt that she had gained a better knowledge of the political and cultural events of the world from her background.[43]

Talk to an MK, and he or she will tell you that they would not trade being an MK for anything. But what about how MKs view their parents' work, how they

become involved, and how they experience God's call to
return as missionaries themselves. Let's take a look. You
will find it very interesting!

Notes

1. Don A. Reavis to William C. Viser, Feb. 12, 1981.
2. Ibid.
3. H. Victor Davis to William C. Viser, Oct. 1, 1981.
4. The Foreign Mission Board of the Southern Baptist Convention, "The Appointment Process," mimeographed, Department of Personnel, 1980.
5. Interview with William A. (Billy) Krushwitz, 27 Jan. 1983.
6. Mary Jane Welch Turner, "Contempo Interview I; Louis R. Cobbs, Billy Krushwitz, and Don Reavis," *Contempo* Mar. 1980, p. 14.
7. The Foreign Mission Board of the Southern Baptist Convention, "Physician's Physical Examination Form for Children," mimographed, Department of the Medical Consultant, 1980.
8. Don A. Reavis to William C. Viser, 20 May 1981.
9. Ibid.
10. Henry A. Holland to William C. Viser, 12 Oct. 1981.
11. Ibid.
12. Reavis to Viser, 20 May 1981.
13. Ibid.
14. Foreign Mission Board of the Southern Baptist Convention, "Instructions for Writing Your Personal History," mimeographed, Department of Personnel, n.d.
15. Interview with Billy Krushwitz, 24 Jan. 1983.
16. Betty More to William C. Viser, 21 Dec. 1981.
17. Truman S. Smith, "Missionary Families: Human and Heroic," *Home Life*, June 1980, pp. 28-29.
18. Edmund Wilson, *The Wound and the Bow* (New York: Oxford University Press, 1965), p. 86.
19. William G. Tanner, "Strictly Personal for Parents of MKs" (unpublished).
20. Richard Rahe, *Feel Younger, Live Longer* (New York: Rand Publishing Company, 1977), p. 80.
21. Franklin Fowler, "The Third World Culture of the MK," *The Commission*, Dec. 1970, p. 1.
22. Ruth Fowler, "The MK Perspective: Growing Up Overseas," *Contempo*, July 1976, pp. 10-11.
23. Franklin Fowler, "The Third World Culture of the MK," *The Commission*, Dec. 1970, p. 1.
24. Editors of *Reader's Digest, Organize Yourself* (New York: Reader's Digest Press, 1982), p. 248.
25. Sophia Gomes, "Research on Missionary Kids," mimiographed, Gardner-Webb College, Boiling Springs, North Car., 1972, pp. 17-20.

26. Laura S. Lane, "Missionary Kids Share Their Feelings AboutBeing MKs," mimeographed, Carson-Newman College, Jefferson City,Tenn. 1976, p. 2.

27. Ibid.

28. Ibid., pp. 5-6.

29. Ibid., p. 6.

30. Ibid.

31. William C. Viser, "A Psychological Profile of Missionary Children in College and the Relationship of Intense Group Therapy to Weekly Group Therapy in the Treatment of Personality Problems as Reflected by the Minnesota Multiphasic Personality Inventory," Ed.D. dissertation, Southwestern Baptist Theological Seminary, 1978, pp. 42-45.

32. Ward, "MK Letters," p. 13.

33. W. David Lockard, "MKs—Call Them Winners," *Accent,* June 1975, p. 6.

34. Betty Cummins, "Growing Up in East Africa," *The Commission,* July 1976, p. 39.

35. Thomas P. Gleason, "The Overseas—Experienced American Adolescent and Patterns of World Mindedness," *Adolescents 8,* (Winter 1973) p. 486.

36. Ruth Fowler, "Just a Title," *The Commission,* Apr. 1975, p. 18.

37. Elizabeth Swadley, "MKs Away from Home," *Royal Service,* Jan. 1977, p. 27.

38. Teresa Shields, "They Share a Common Heritage," *The Commission,* 1976, p. 10.

39. Kendra Smith, "MK Letters," *Accent,* Apr. 1975, p. 21.

40. Ward, "MK Letters," p. 27.

41. Ibid.

42. Stanley D. Stamps, "MK Roots," *The Commission,* Jan. 1975, p. 6.

43. Teresa Shields, "They Share a Common Heritage," *The Commission,* Mar. 1976, p. 10.

3
Like Parent, Like Child

What kinds of feelings did you have about your parents' work as you grew up? Did you understand what they were doing and how their work affected them positively or negatively? What effect did it have upon your family?

Identification with the Parents' Work

MKs are closely identified with the work of their parents, much more so than their peers in the United States.

You will recall in chapter 2 that 90 percent of the MKs surveyed by Laura Lane responded that *they* would be willing to raise their own children on the foreign mission field. This speaks for a very positive experience. Lane herself feels that this indicates MKs believe in missions and what their parents are doing. She concluded that such a high percentage is quite unusual in any vocation.[1]

The child's identification with the work of his parents begins very early. Cara Sorley, the seven-year-old daughter of David and Darlene Sorley, missionaries to Uganda, told her mother as they talked about the future: "I was thinking that when I grow up, I'd like to get married and come back to Africa and tell the people about Jesus."[2]

I remember a conversation with my own son Ryan, four years old at the time. He was quietly stacking blocks together to form a house. I asked him what he was building, and he responded, "I'm making a WMU building."

It becomes a simple matter for MKs to learn an early identification with the work of their parents. As Americans living overseas, they are frequently asked the question, "Why are you here?"

I believe the identification with the work of an MK's parents is actually twofold.

Perception of Parents' Work

First, it is the MK's perception of how his mother and father view their work.

The Gomes survey asked the question, "Do you think your parents are happy in their position as missionaries?" Twenty-six MKs responded positively, there were no negative responses, and three were unsure.[3]

In my dissertation survey, I included the response "I resent my parents' work" in a list of fourteen problems and asked MKs to check and prioritize the three most common to them. Significantly enough, that statement did not appear in the top three. As a matter of fact, five out of two hundred and thirty-four indicated this as a problem.

In my survey to the missionaries in South Brazil, I asked for a response to this statement:

My child is supportive of my work here.

Ninety-three percent said yes, 4 percent said no, while 3 percent were unsure.

I would conclude the significance of this perception with reference to an article entitled "Missionary Family Behavior, Dissonance, and Children's Career Decision." The author Theodore Hsieh questioned seventy-eight MKs attending four different Christian institutions and drew two conclusions:

1. The missionary career is held in high esteem by the missionary children in the study.

2. They show respect for the values, difficulties, and sacrifices which such a career requires.[4]

Not to be overlooked is his conclusion that the missionary child's perception of his father's (and, of course, mother's) satisfaction with his routine, daily activities related significantly to the MK's decision in choosing a missionary career.[5]

Involvement in Their Parents' Work

Second, it is the MK's actual involvement in the work of their parents that strengthens such a close identification.

I should quickly point out that all MKs are involved, some more so than others, in their parent's work. As reflected in the surveys above, MK after MK expressed to me their overwhelmingly positive attitude towards their parents' work. Consider a few comments.

I'm very thankful that they are missionaries, and I thank God for allowing me to be born in a foreign country.—Kathy Joiner, Ecuador.

I respect their work and am proud of them.—Grace Morris, Taiwan.

I admire and respect my parents for the work they are doing.—Carl Tarry, South Brazil.

Another shared: "I'm grateful that they are missionaries —I've had such a rich life because of it."

Every MK is not able to become involved with their parents' work to the extent desired. This may be due to the nature of their parent's work or the fact that the MK is away in boarding school or attending college in the US.

Nevertheless, several related how they had become involved and how it affected them. Consider these reflections:

I love what my parents are doing, and I wouldn't exchange being an MK with anyone who has lived in the

States all the time. I went with my dad when he preached at villages, and I taught Sunday School at the church in La Cuba. This is so much fun because children in this country show so much innocent, pure love.—Becky Roberts, Honduras.

I am very proud of their work, and I was involved with their work. My father works with book stores and literature. I would help display books at fairs, camps, etc.—David Gregory, Mexico.

I grew up in Costa Rica. I feel like their job was very worthwhile and very appreciated by their national co-workers. I was actively involved in teaching as well as Sunday School by age eight and was in charge of the nursery by age eleven. I feel good about my contribution.—Karen Lynn Doyle, Guatemala.

I felt that my dad and mom were achieving a lot in sharing the gospel. I'd help out in leading the singing in some services. Generally all of my sisters, my brother, and I were involved in the church services.—Mike McClelland, Rhodesia.

I am proud of what my parents are doing in Japan. Because I was away at boarding school most of the time I did not get too involved, but when I was home on weekends I was able to teach Sunday School classes in the Sunday School we started in our home.—Grace Emanual, Japan.

Many MKs commented that they were active in their local church in various leadership capacities; others shared experiences of accompaning parents on preaching or medical missions. Others shared in assisting parents with setting up slide projectors, secretarial work in the seminary, and in many other ways.

Some MKs did not participate as they wish they had. One MK shared, "I was not involved, but I think their work is something I should have been participating in."

Another shared, "I was involved in their work somewhat —now that I look back on it, I regret I didn't get more involved."

. MKs are definitely a part of their parent's work. I like the way Jonja Ann Deal, MK from Jordan, stated it:

I love the work Mom and Dad do because (1) it is God's will for their lives, and (2) it's what they're happy doing—what they want to do! I was never really old enough to really be a part of Mom and Dad's actual work but I feel like, in retrospect, that I had an influence and played a part whether I knew it or not.

Having heard from the MKs, let's hear how parents involved their children in the work. Many and varied are the ways in which MKs are involved in their parents work.

When I sent out the survey worldwide to my missionary collegues asking them if they involved their children in their work, 83 percent responded yes, 15 percent no, and 2 percent were unsure.

Many mentioned over and over again that their children were involved as "door openers." Through interest in them as light-skinned, blonde-haired children, their parents were able to witness. It reminds me so much of Isaiah 11:6, "A little child shall lead them."

Not all MKs are involved in the work of their parents as much as the parents might desire. Just as there was regret expressed on the part of some MKs looking backward and wishing they had been more involved, there are also missionary parents who regret that their children were not or are not more involved.

One father expressed this when he said, "They have worked in VBS and been interested in our work by degrees. The first child had less interest, the second a little more, but the last two have high interest. I can't explain why it is like this."

Children of all ages become involved with their parents
—some at a very early age.

Mike Glenn, doing seminary extension work in
Venezuela, often took seven-year-old Aaron with him as
he traveled and taught. Mike said, "I share with him what
I do, and he sees it firsthand."

Robert Horner goes to rural churches in Chile to
preach. When his daughter Julie was seven, she often
went with him to pass out tracts and participate in street
evangelism.

Medically speaking, MKs find ample opportunities.

Dr. Sam Cannata of Sudan shared that Mike and Cathy
helped in the clinic, while Stanley spent time getting a
house ready for new missionaries.

The Loregrens, missionaries to Jordan where he serves
as a physician, related that their children, Miriam and
Linda, served as hospital volunteers.

Mrs. Lee Baggett from Mexico wrote that their twelve-
year-old daughter, Dhana, participated in clinics at least
once a year translating and helping dentists while the
Overtons of Barbados, West Indies, involve their three,
Todd, Chad, and Lainie, in much the same way. They
travel with them to dental clinics where they help regis-
ter patients.

Dr. Dean Fitzgerald, Jr., a physician in Gaza, stated that
his oldest son is a scrub technician having learned in the
operating room there.

Other MKs become quite involved in the evangelistic
work which is so important.

Phil and Oretha Brewster of the Philippines jointly
shared that watching their children pray for a friend and
seeing that friend make a decision was a time of rejoicing
for the whole family.

Mrs. Pat Wolf of Taiwan related that her youngest son,
John, when he was eight was so enthusiastic about sharing

the gospel that he and another MK handed out over 1,000 tracts, even flagging down a taxi and a police car to give them a tract.

The David Parkers of Zambia are very involved in church development work and take their two young daughters, Melanie and Anne, with them. They pass out tracts with their parents throughout their travels.

The Loren Turnages of Scotland have seen their children involved in setting up and operating a movie projector, helping in VBS, assisting in driving to various locations, passing out tracts, and being faithful in young people's activities locally.

Manny and Becky Manferd of Chile are involved in teaching classes of adults. Their children, Cory and Melissa, play with the children of the adults attending the class and entertain them until the class is over.

The Fred Leurets of Nigeria shared that their oldest son, Stan, helped with bookkeeping while their daughters, Susan and Jan, helped sew school uniforms for a Baptist High School. Scott, along with his brothers and sisters, made bush trips with his parents, helped to set up camp, and assisted in the evangelistic meetings.

Many MKs become involved through use of musical talents. One missionary mother mentioned that her daughter started her musical career by playing the little pump organ in their small church.

The Ray Registers of Israel stated that their three— Chuck, Jimmy, and Cheryl—rang handbells in a bell choir.

The Don McNeelys of Zambia have a children's television program and their three—Rob, Wes and Bart—help them with the puppets.

When all is said and done, I do not believe it is a matter of whether MKs participate in the work of their parents.

They all do, directly or indirectly, actively or passively. They cannot help but influence their parents' work.

One missionary mother put it this way: "As younger children, their love and affection was noticed more than once by the nationals."

Erik Erikson asserted that a background of love and trust is fundamental.[6] Without this the child's chances of becoming a reasonably happy, effective, contributing adult and of developing a positive self-image and a sense of his own identity are seriously impaired, as clinical experience and any number of more systematic investigations make abundantly clear.[7]

MKs know this background and have many opportunities to make meaningful contributions. No one can know the full impact of this upon the work of their parents.

Mrs. Gerald Workman of Malawi shared an incident which is appropriate here. Their two MKs. Philip and Deborah, usually give gifts of toys and clothes at Christmas to their Malawian playmates. When Deborah was four, she gave stuffed animals from her collection to eight little girls in the neighborhood. On Christmas morning as the family walked to church, they saw these little girls with their new toys tied on their backs just as their mothers tied their babies on their backs.

Another incident which also speaks of love was shared by Mrs. Janice Corington of Ghana, West Africa. She will tell it in her own words.

Our "Sunday night place" happened to be under a big tree in the TB village on the hospital grounds. People from many different tribes met with us for Sunday night worship. Although there is a fine building up the road a bit, we all preferred the benches sitting under the tree. The only inconvenience in this situation was that sometimes there weren't enough benches for everyone and that meant latecomers and children sat on the ground.

Our two daughters, Karen and Julie, preferred this worship place to any they have encountered in Africa. I am sure one of the reasons was that the children there adored them.

One Sunday night we were squeezed together on the benches singing and clapping. A small Falani girl about five years of age had managed to have the seat of honor next to Julie. This didn't last long though because an older child came up and demanded that the smaller Falani girl give up her seat. Because the child was of the Falani tribe there was no protest. I knew there would not be any objections raised by the adults in the circle either. Prejudice abounds the world over, and it had now raised its ugly head under our tree. Because there was no more space on the benches the only seat available was on the ground. The little girl had been one of the first arrivals, and this seemed so unfair. She looked hurt and bewildered standing in the middle of the circle, but she didn't have to stay there long! Out of the corner of my eye I could see Karen and Julie shifting around. There was enough space *between* them for one little Falani girl. I didn't know my daughters had realized the significance of what they had done until Julie looked around at me and grinned. There were two sermons preached that night: One by my husband and one by my daughters.

Missionary families grow together. They learn to love one another more, and they learn to love the nationals more as well. They grow and mature physically, and they grow spiritually.

Jasper McPhail, a former missionary doctor in India, and currently chairman of the surgery department at Oral Roberts University School of Medicine, Tulsa, Oklahoma, stated, "The inner spiritual life is my resource here and there. Spiritual growth comes from staying in the Word, in fellowship and in witnessing. . . . Priorities in one's responsibilities have to be determined in prayer."[8]

The Tallmans of Europe add that the only real strength of any family is the strength of Jesus Christ. "We found we really had to stay within hearing range of the Lord—all five of us—because the Lord doesn't just instruct the parents; he has some valuable things to teach us through our kids."9

MKs teach their parents many things, but they also learn from their parents, as well. They learn to pray and witness. They learn about the Jesus their parents have come to tell others about, and they learn to grow in their faith.

Kendra Smith of Malaysia shared very personally:

The travel and opportunities of living overseas are great privileges, but the most fascinating part of being an MK, I think, is to see God at work in people who have never before heard of him. All of us, wherever we are, can see God working, but I've been able to see a close-up view of the way God works in missions. I've found that being this close has really helped me in my own spiritual growth. There was a time when I felt that God was being pushed at me, but the feeling didn't last long and wasn't very strong. All I had to do was make a stronger commitment to Christ myself.

I would like to share an experience I've just had and how God has really worked through it here in Malaysia. On August 10, 1974, my fifteen-year-old brother was killed in a bicycle-car accident. This was the most tragic experience I've ever faced because Scott and I were very close. God has given me so much strength. There are very few Christians at school, and Scott and I had tried to witness to the kids. After his death five of these were saved, including two for whom Scott had been very concerned. Three out of the five were saved at the funeral by Scott's grave. To me this was a victory that God promised in 1 Corinthians 15:58. I think there will be many more victories that come from this. I just praise the Lord for all he has done!

I enjoy being an MK and I wouldn't trade places with anyone. All of us can experience the greatness of God and His joy, and I just pray that everyone can be happy with what He was given in life. As one of my friends always says, "The beauty is in the eyes of the beholder." I think we can all find beauty where we are if we look for it.[10]

Consideration of a Church-Related Career

MKs are beautiful people in the best sense of the word. They learn of missions firsthand, and many will make decisions to enter church related vocations or will return to the foreign country where they have grown up to be missionaries themselves. Others will go different directions. I believe MKs are sensitive to God's leadership whatever it may be. I believe the following MKs speak for the majority in what they shared with me when I asked them the question, "Have you decided, or are you considering a church-related career at this point?"

No, although I plan to be a missionary wherever I am.—Joy Turner, South Brazil.

Yes and no. Actually, I am going to leave the final decision up to God, and I'll do whatever He wants me to.—Doug Eaton, Tanzania.

I don't know if my career will be *church* oriented. I do hope for it to be oriented toward Jesus Christ.—Florence Lusk, Hong Kong.

Other MKs feel God's call to church related and other vocations within the United States:

I have decided upon medicine here in the United States. I feel that it is related to reaching out to others and helping them. Mom and Dad have set an example for me.—Ruth Roberts, Kenya.

I am *considering* a church-related career, perhaps because of my experience overseas as an MK and being around church-related (career) people.—Jeffrey Divers, Argentina.

At this point I am considering a church-related career, but I am not sure yet just what God wants me to do. One major factor has been growing up on the mission field, seeing the great need for workers.—Delana West, Venezuela.

Yes, I am considering a church-related career. Significant factors have been that my development as a Christian has led me to consider any kind of service, but I have been more drawn to areas of need where others are less willing to go. My exposure to overseas missionary service has also helped to broaden my understanding.—Bradley Beevers, Indonesia.

I will be going into the ministry. The Lord has brought me to this point after years of preparation through people, circumstances, experiences, etc.—especially through other missionaries and their experiences.—Stephen James, East Asia.

The MK's Call to Foreign Missions

Other MKs feel God's call for foreign missions as they return overseas following college and seminary preparation to proclaim and spread the gospel.

Several factors emerge as having influenced their decision for missions.

1. A keen awareness of the existing needs overseas. Bill Reynolds of Belgium said, "I cannot possibly ignore the call to foreign missions after being so much a part of it. The need is so great, but the workers are few."

Paige Reece of Nigeria related a commitment to overseas work but is still seeking God's direction. He also points to the need factor as he wrote: "I am so conscious of the need of the people, and I cannot sit back in the US in peace."

2. The model of the parents and their love for the work.

Mark Romoser of Argentina addresses both the first and second factors in his thoughts:

"I am considering being a preacher and possibly even a missionary. I believe the fact that my father does this is very significant, but I have also been influenced by the need I see around the world, especially where I lived."

3. An existing deep love for the people of the country where the MK was raised.

Vera Hern of Jordan shared, "I have prayed about going to the mission field. The reason I have considered this is because of my love for the Middle East and the people there."

4. A recognition of the talents and skills God has given to them.

John Beyget of Taiwan feels drawn to serving overseas as a business manager for a mission and relates that he "feels God's calling as a result of his recognition of need and my own talent in the area of business."

God works in *many* and through many different circumstances to make His will known and His call plain.

Mark Smith of Indonesia expressed his consideration of God's call in these words, so simple yet so profound:

"Yes, I am seriously considering missions. I feel that I wish to do something for God, and this is the greatest thing I can do."

God's call to MKs leads them back to the foreign field into all areas of mission work. Consider these five:

Religious Education: One of my majors is religious education. I chose this to be one of my majors because I am planning to go back to Korea as a missionary.—Pam Wootton, Korea.

Student Work: I am considering doing student work overseas. I feel comfortable working in a Christian vocation because of my parents.—Jonathan Kirkendall, Belgium.

Education: I am considering being a teacher in a school for MKs overseas because I got a good education myself. I think that's important.—Lori Hope, South Brazil.

Social Work: I am considering sociological work among

the youth in churches overseas. Foreign Mission Week in Glorieta influenced this decision a great deal.—Jeff Bailey, Argentina.

The Journeyman Program: I feel the Lord is leading me to be a journeyman for two years. Besides that I am still looking and praying.

These are but a few of many areas of mission work that Mks will go into with great zeal and enthusiasm.

MKs are no different from their US peers in terms of responding to God's will. God has a plan for every young person, MK or not. He requires obedience of us all.

I am reminded of what one MK wrote after expressing her desire to do God's will, whatever it might be. She said, "Pray for me, please." This request should speak to all of us.

As we have examined MKs' identification and participation with the work of their parents and their effects upon the MKs future vocational plans, let's now turn our attention to what it is like to grow up in a foreign country, how different cultures positively and negatively affect MKs' development, dating in a foreign culture, and how MKs have used their leisuretime and hobbies in some rather uniqueways to witness to others.

Notes

1. Laura S. Lane, "Missionary Kids Share Their Feelings About Being MKs," Mimeographed, Carson-Newman College, Jefferson City, Tenn., 1976, p. 6.

2. Robert O'Brien, "Looking Ahead," *The Commission,* Feb.-Mar. 1983, p. 5.

3. Sophia Regina Gomes, "Research On Missionary Kids," Mimeographed, Gardner-Webb College, Boiling Springs, NC, 1972, p. 17.

4. Theodore Hsich, "Missionary Family Behavior, Dissonance, and Children's Career Decisions," *Journal of Psychology and Theology* 4 (Summer 1976), p. 226.

5. Ibid.

6. Erik H. Erikson, *Identity: Youth and Crisis* (New York: Norton Co., 1968), p. 127.

7. John J. Conger, *Adolescence and Youth* (New York: Harper and Row, 1973), p. 196.

8. Martha Skelton, "Missionary Families: Some Stresses and Strengths," *The Commission*, Dec. 1981, p. 13.

9. Ibid.

10. Kendra Smith, "MK Letters," *Accent*, Apr. 1975, p. 21.

Uganda—MK Cara Soreley holds one of the teaching aids during a worship service. FMB photo by Warren Johnson.

Spain—MK Kari Henry teaches a Sunday School Class. FMB photo by Larry Henry.

Brazil—MK Susie Sharpley taught retarded adults as a Mission Service Corps volunteer. FMB photo by Don Rutledge.

Burkina Faso—MKs Jason and Cory Foster listen on front row as their father Jim preaches. FMB photo by Joanna Pinneo.

Brazil—Jimmy Moon conducts a Bible study with a Brazilian family. FMB photo by Don Rutledge.

Bangladesh—MK Jamie Young and her mother talk with a mother and her son from the Magura Baptist Church family. FMB photo by Don Rutledge.

Ecuador—MK Debbie Wyatt (second from right) in class at Alliance Academy. FMB photo by Don Rutledge.

Burkina Faso—MKs Cory and Jason have math class with their mom Dorothy Foster. FMB photo by Mark Snowden.

Uganda—MK Bo Goodgame (center) participates in French Class at Lincoln School. FMB photo by Warren Johnson.

MK Kelly Parris (far left) is part of a GA meeting at Orientation Center in Pine Mountain, Georgia. FMB photo by Ken Lawson.

Liberia—MKs Timmy and Jonnie Hill play basketball at MK hostel in Monrovia. FMB photo by Joanna Pinneo.

Indonesia—Don and Sarah Duvall play ball with their daughters, Ellen and Ruth. FMB photo by Don Rutledge.

Kenya—MK Jay Richardson learns to play tee ball with father and friends looking on. FMB photo by Warren Johnson.

Nigeria—MKs Elizabeth and Grace Hall at the piano at Baptist Pastors School in Kaduna. FMB photo by Joanna Pinneo.

Colombia—MK Michael Wyatt (right), director of Thomas Jefferson School, talks with his father Roy. FMB photo by Don Rutledge.

Group activities during an MK Thanksgiving weekend at Camp Hanover in Richmond, Virginia. FMB photo by Paul Brock.

4
Growing Up in Another Culture

Can you imagine what it would be like to grow up outside of the United States and spend your developmental years in another country and another culture? MKs are people who do. They are the product of two cultures, the American culture of their parents and the foreign culture where they are living. For this reason they are sometimes referred to as "third culture people."

We have already seen the positive feelings MKs hold toward growing up in another culture and all of its many benefits in the previous three chapters. Those benefits plus existing negative factors will contribute immeasurably to the MK's ever-developing personality.

In fact one writer compared the organization of a personality to the organization of culture. To him, culture is the sum total of the ways people pattern their functions.[1]

It is also important to see culture as a process in which personalities affected by long periods of association express themselves in generally acceptable ways. The intruder into this "function of personalities" may be rejected or accepted according to the "function of personalities" of which culturally he has been a part.[2]

In other words, culture determines what is acceptable and what is not acceptable for the person of that culture to do. The MK, as a Christian young person, brings into his adjustment within that foreign culture all that he has learned about Christianity. His growing personality will be determined by his ever-growing faith and Christian convictions, his family, and that foreign culture to name but a few of the dynamics. How similar or dissimilar that foreign culture is to the culture of the United States may make the difference between an easier adjustment in the future to the US and a more difficult one. Let me point out that I am certainly not stating as a matter of fact that a dissimilar culture is a hard-and-fast predictor of future adjustment problems. Too many MKs from these different cultures could dispell that idea, and in chapter 5 I want to examine what missionary parents are doing and what the average layperson can do to make the US adjustment easier for the MK.

Nonetheless, the similarity or difference in the foreign culture and the culture of the United States is not without its influence upon the personality development of the MK and his future adjustment in the US.

Let's look at the matter of identification of the MK with the national or foreign culture of which he is a part.

Franklin Fowler observed that MKs can be placed into three groups as far as this identification is concerned.[3]

1. The first group would be those from Africa. Here there is very little difficulty in identification since the MKs identify very much with the American culture. They are raised somewhat in isolation from the national culture, go to MK schools which are basically American or British oriented, so that they really have very little difficulty with identification.

The Middle East would probably be more like the African grouping.

2. Those in South America, especially if they were born there or went at an early age, tend to identify very closely with the national culture, language, and nationals. I know that even now part of me is Latin American. [Franklin Fowler's parents were

missionaries in Argentina where he grew up.] I still thrill to see the blue, white, and blue flag of Argentina and still enjoy speaking Spanish. As you know, most of the Brazilian MKs, especially when they come to the States, are ready to shed blood for Brazil. Though this may not be exactly what the parents would want, there is not too much difficulty with identification.

Europe would probably be identified with South America.

3. The third group would be those MKs having grown up, generally speaking, in the Orient. Here I believe there is confusion of identification. For one thing the national culture, though on the surface, many times is somewhat Western; basically, it is not. Thus it seems that the MKs do have a harder time of identifying in the Orient. They are not quite sure just who they are, and it has been my observation that we probably have more difficulty with adjustment difficulties of youngsters in the Orient than in the other two areas.[3]

Yet, he feels that, "as a whole, I really think that our children (MKs) adapt quite well, and I would dare say that if we had a way of comparing the problems that our adolescent MKs develop on the mission field to an equal peer group—say here in the States—we would find that our MKs probably do much better."[4]

There is no question in my judgment about Fowler's observations. Part of my doctoral dissertation gave me the opportunity to test a representative number of MKs using the Minnesota Multiphasic Personality Inventory (MMPI) as my instrument. This psychological inventory according to authorities in the field "has come to occupy a unique place among objective measurements of personality characteristics."[5] Another adds that it is the most elaborate and complete instrument in this field,[6] while still another states that "in addition to having stimulated extensive research it holds the distinction of being the most widely used personality inventory."[7]

Thirty-five MKs attending colleges and universities in

Texas were invited to take the MMPI. This group represented twenty-two different countries throughout the world. Provisions were made to prevent the classification of the MK (freshman, sophmore, junior, or senior) and the sex from rendering the test results meaningless. The MMPI scores of the MKs were then compared to an established table of test scores from college students across the United States considered to be stable and normal. There was no difference in the two.[8]

MKs learn to relate to the world from their unique third culture background, not entirely the culture of their parents (A) nor completely that of the foreign country in which they live (B) but what one called a "C pattern." This means that a diplomat's son reared in Indonesia will have more in common with a missionary kid from the Congo than he will with the average American in Indonesia.[9]

Overall, as already indicated, MKs consider their third culture to be a big plus in their personality development. Just as this third culture is unique, so are many of its dynamics that contribute to the shaping of the MK's personality. Consider these factors.

Contributing Factors to Personality Development

"Americanness" of the MK

Some MKs were born in the United States and lived there for several years prior to their parents' appointment. They may relate and develop within the culture differently as a result of those prior years in the US.

Other MKs are born on the mission field or go to the field at such an early age that they have no real memories of their very early years in the US. The foreign culture is the only culture they really know.

Regardless of which category an MK comes from, he or

she will have to deal with their "Americanness" as their personality grows and develops within their given culture. What do I mean by "Americanness"? Let's consider this from several angles.

As a preface, the fact that the MK's parents are Americans, with the sending agency (The Foreign Mission Board) located in the USA, the MK's citizenship (many countries allow a child to hold dual citizenship until a certain age when he has to choose which of the two countries he will claim), and his physical appearance (depending on that of the foreign culture) readily identify the MK as "an American." This is not without great significance.

Physical. From a physical point of view, the MK will quickly learn that his appearance is different from that of the people in his foreign land.

Brenda (Mrs. Doug) Ringer of Thailand voiced this well in referring to her three boys—Joshua, Steven, and Matthew: "Our young children are touched, pinched, etc. in the markets because the Thais think they are lovely."

We saw earlier that the MK often opens the door for his parents to witness simply from the attraction and difference of his physical appearance, but—consider the reward that the Ringers have seen in their boys as they have had to deal with this "difference"—"it has taught our boys patience."

This illustrates but one of many positive lessons that both parents and MKs pointed out.

Social. From a social point of view the MK is not living in the United States. He only returns once every several years, depending upon which "furlough option" his parents choose. Many dynamics will determine how closely an MK will identify with that foreign culture. Sometimes the closeness of that identification even surprises the MK himself. Consider the college freshman who grew up in Europe.

"I had fooled myself into thinking I was an American through and through (fair skin, blue eyes, blond hair), but I was surprised to find what little I had in common with Americans."

For some the identification may be more obvious.

"I think, act, and live like a Spaniard. I am an American by nationality (that is, passport, social security, and so forth), but in my heart I am definitely a Spaniard. You can take me out of Spain, but you can't take Spain out of me. It is hard to explain this to relatives."

MK James Hagood, having grown up in an Eastern culture, relates his identification with two cultures in these terms. "I feel as if I am 100 percent American and 100 percent Lebanese."[10]

This identification does not come without the struggle that many MKs face.

When asked if belonging to two worlds at the same time had ever been a source of discomfort, he responded, "Many times. Trying to live up to the expectations of both can be difficult. As a teenager searching for identity, I was often torn between the two styles of life."[11]

For some, the language will become a barrier that will influence the identification. As one missionary related, "Living with people all the time whom you cannot talk to is tough on a child. Our foreign language is difficult."

As you read in chapter 1, some MKs will leave home early to attend boarding school. This may bring about more of an American identification due to association and living with American students in a school run by Americans.

Economic. From an economic point of view an MK living in a foreign culture will, at times, consciously or subconsciously relate, compare, and contrast it with that of the United States.

One MK shared, "Growing up in my country has given

me a better understanding of how good God has been to America."

Other MKs related in other ways: Robert Nash, Jr., of the Philippines, "I am so much more aware of waste, etc."

Janell Smith of Jordan, "[I am] more conserving of energy and water."

Still others would feel that being "a rich American" prevents some from relating to them.

There are a few observations that need to be made at this point.

There will always exist the myth among some that their missionaries are "living in the lap of luxury" or "high on the hog."

I cannot forget the businessman who approached me one Sunday morning prior to our departure to begin missionary orientation and said, "I wouldn't give a penny to foreign missions. You missionaries really live it up." That mentality hurts all the way around. It hurts him because he misses the blessings and the joy of giving to see others won to Christ, and, most of all, he hurts Christ himself since he has disassociated himself with the Great Commission in Matthew 28:19-20.

In a sense, missionaries are "rich Americans." We have more as Americans—period—than do most people of other countries. You are reminded of this every day as you read your newspapers and watch the news on television.

Everyday people from other countries come to America to live and settle down. They want to share in that abundance with which we have been blessed.

You never understand how the world sees your country until you live overseas. The influence of our movies and television programs exported to other countries is staggering!

I remember a young man who approached me after our Sunday School class one morning with a question. He

knew that we would be leaving for Texas to begin our first
furlough, and he had watched several episodes of a popular television series. His question to me was, "Is every
family in Texas like the ones I see on television?"

Still another that comes to mind involved young adults
in US State Department projects working in other countries. They would go into villages to work with and help
village people of great poverty. At night they set up a
projector and shared some episodes of a popular television series to entertain the people. The series featured a
"talking horse" who lived in an air-conditioned, paneled,
beautifully furnished stable. A missionary friend explained that the natives were dumbfounded. Even a horse
in the US lived in such luxury!

Missionaries live with this stereotype of luxury in their
foreign countries, and in a sense of abundance as it is for
all of us, it is true; but in the sense of becoming wealthy
or "living like kings," nothing could be further from the
truth.

How much do missionaries make? The Foreign Mission
Board strives to pay its missionaries a salary equal to that
of what the average Southern Baptist pastor receives. In-
surance, retirement benefits, health coverage, educational assistance to children, and other considerations
compose the package. The Foreign Mission Board intends
for this to be sufficient for the missionary to live adequate-
ly. Neither he nor his wife may undertake employment
beyond their missionary work. Their work as a missionary
is to be their full responsibility with all that it implies.

The size of the house they live in has already been
determined by the FMB in a guideline referred to earlier.
In addition, the mission itself will largely determine the
car he drives and where the missionary will live.

When economic conditions destabilize the local curren-
cy, and the dollar is strengthened, the Board makes a

correction and will make whatever cuts are necessary to bring the salary back into line. This is to ensure that missionaries all over the world will be paid equally.

Missionaries respond to God's call to spread the gospel, not because of material benefits. We go in obedience to Him. Our response is no different than what God expects of all His children. We are enabled to do His work through the thousands upon thousands who give joyfully and obediently, from the youngest child with his pennies, nickels, and dimes to those able to give far more. We are provided for, and I will always be grateful, as is my missionary family, to God and His people for making our work possible. However, to think that a missionay is deriving great material gain and living in luxury is both untrue and unfair.

All missionaries and MKs deal with the abundance all of us have, and yet it takes on a unique and different perspective when you are an American living among those who have so little. Martha (Mrs. Cordell) Akin of Tanzania said it well, "Just accepting the wealth that is ours by being American has been a hard adjustment but good for character building. It's hard for all of us to be 'rich' in a poor country."

One last aspect of the economic influence concerns the MK coping within a country where his peers may be sons and daughters of very affluent Americans, Europeans, or others who represent businesses there. These peers will have access to money, clothes, and items from the US that the MK does not. Their parents may not be concerned with living a Christian life-style. Thus the MK learns to relate to those, who might know little or perhaps nothing about Christianity.

Political: From a political point of view, missionaries live in ever-changing environments, some more than others. What would it be like to grow and develop in a country in turmoil? Consider these descriptions.

From Lebanon: "We have been living in a war zone with pressures on everyone." Although this missionary felt that the children developed well emotionally in spite of the turmoil, one wrote, "It could have just as easily been destructive."

Dorris (Mrs. Harry B.) Garvin of Uganda shared about her children's growth and development: "They have had to really depend more on God for peace and security as their life was threatened in Uganda during Idi Amin's rule. Then after they went to Kenya to boarding school they knew God was watching over Mom and Dad and little sisters as well."

Yvonne (Mrs. David G.) Parker of Zambia related in a similar vein: "We came into Zambia when the country was involved with the war in Rhodesia (now Zimbabwe). Melanie, at the age of six and seven, had to deal with fear and learn to go to God in prayer each and every time she was afraid. I did not need to do this for myself until I was a teenager."

Intellectual. From an intellectual, spiritual, and emotional point of view, being an American can be the means of accepting responsibility early. Majorie (Mrs. Howard D.) Olive of the Philippines stated, "I think our children became more mature emotionally at a more rapid pace because Filipinos naturally look to Americans for leadership. They were pushed early to be leaders."

People and Their Typical Life-Style

We learned in chapter 2 that how a culture views the family will have an influence upon the missionary family. It will also plant this cultural concept and others as well within the MK. Consider just a few of the benefits learned from another culture.

The African people have an amazing capacity for suffering. They are blessed with a great patience and a profound appreciation for the simple things of life. It was good for the girls to see firsthand that man's pleasures do not consist in what you possess.—Charles and Betty Whitson, South West Africa.

The country of Argentina is very family oriented. There is not such a separation of activities regarding youth, adults, and senior citizens. Everyone joins in together for many things. I see this as a healthy and beneficial experience for them.—Annette (Mrs. Robert W.) Crockett, Argentina.

In Leslie's school there are twenty-one countries represented, in Doug's preschool (out of fifteen kids) there are six countries represented. They also see the world as it is: hunger, shortages, people in real need, and as we try to live a 'simple life-styles' they are aware of what they can do to help. They give their clothes and toys to needy friends.—Suzanne (Mrs. V. Lynn) Groce, Ethiopia.

Our six-year-old, Morgan, seems to have a great compassion for the poor as he sees beggars and refugees in need daily and often goes with us as we take food and clothing to these people.—Janet (Mrs. William R.) Swan, Hong Kong.

Still another missionary wife shared, "They [the children] respect elders because they were taught to and also because it is very much a part of the Arab culture. They also adjusted and are happy to dress according to the extremely modest dress code of the Arab culture."

And after hearing from the parents, let's hear from some MKs who speak for many others.

I grew up with Africans, and a lot of their reasons and beliefs are cemented into my mind.—Belenda Senter, Tanzania.

[I have a] greater respect for elders and an understanding of cultural differences without racial prejudice.—Paul Hollis, Hong Kong.

It has helped me realize the real situation of the world and how lucky I am to have lived in two cultures. It has helped me to take the best of my two cultures to set up my own values and goals.—Robert Carter, Chile.

I think of people as people, all having some basic needs and feelings. I don't let culture, color, or other differences stand in the way.—Cathy Hardy, Japan.

Nonexistent Basic "Rites of Passage"

Have you ever considered the influence exerted on your development of such basic, life-changing circumstances as having a job or getting a driver's license?

In many countries, MKs are not allowed to drive as early as their peers in the US. Some MKs feel this absence strongly in their foreign culture. If they could drive, they would likely not be able to afford a car since other countries do not have the automobile market that we have in the US, and the cost would far exceed what the MK could pay.

To be employed would also be most difficult in some countries where laws and circumstances are different and perhaps where unemployment already exists at high levels.

Young people in the US look forward to and take for granted these opportunities and others; but for the most part, MKs do not and experience them only when in the US for furloughs with their parents or while attending college.

Cultural Viewpoint of the Masculine and Feminine Sex

It goes without saying that there often exists great prejudice in a foreign country for one sex and against another. MKs must often deal with this at an early age even before they are aware of what it is all about.

For example, consider the male child and his preferential treatment.

Some friends of ours related how their three-year-old son was told to pick up his toys in the presence of a young Latin American woman who was helping take care of him. When he did not do as they asked, his father disciplined him, and the boy began to cry. The young Latin American woman seemed upset but said nothing. Later on the parents noticed a continued improvement in their son's room. They later discovered why. They told him to pick up a toy he had left on the floor. Rather than do it himself, he stamped his foot, pointed his finger, and speaking in the national language said, "Maria, you do it!"

When I asked a group of teenage MKs to mention some problems they had encountered in adjusting while living in a Latin American culture, some of the girls mentioned prejudices towards women. This same answer came from another, but, in this case, she was brought up under a Muslim influence where her parents were missionaries. She expressed:

"My view of women here in the US is lower because of the Muslim influence, so I strive to prove myself worthy of attention and love as a girl."

Difference in Educational Opportunities

Have you ever thought about the influence that colleges and universities exert upon the lives of children and teenagers throughout the US?

They serve as locations for various activities that draw kids of all ages. It may be an athletic event where kids can meet the players and/or watch a game, a visit to a planetarium, or a special children's play sponsored by the drama department. It might serve as a location for a sum-

mer youth camp, and, of course, all universities either
have special weekends for high school students or encourage them to visit the campus.

The MK does not grow up with this kind of influence.
His opportunity to see the college he is to attend might
take place as early as the tenth grade. The next time he
returns home it will be to begin college. There are no
opportunities to visit several unless that MK does so while
on furlough or makes a special trip to the US.

Some MKs mention this as one frustration in their experience overseas.

Protectiveness

Depending upon the culture in which the MK lives,
some will readily stand apart from their peers in the host
country due to their skin, eyes, hair, or even their height.
Others will not, and it may be impossible to distinguish
them from their peers even in their speech. Nevertheless,
the potential exists for differences to be noticed.

One couple shared with us during recent tensions within their country and the kidnapping of some Americans
that they had instructed their teenagers to speak only the
foreign language while on the streets.

We have already seen that the type of boarding school
may create a very protective environment which shelters
the MK from things that his peers have faced for years.

For example, while speaking at a youth retreat toward
the end of our furlough in 1983, an eighth-grade student
shared with the group that he had seen fourth- and fifth-
grade students smoking marijuana in the elementary
school restroom.

Yet an MK, a freshman in college, told me that he had
never been faced with a drug problem throughout his
high school experience. He really felt he had been "living
in a bubble."

This certainly is not the rule but is a distinct possibility for the MK in the right circumstances.

Franklin Fowler addressed this dilemma when he wrote: Since cultures are different and many times morals are on a different level, the missionary parents tend to want to " 'protect' their children from the surrounding environment. That this needs to be done I would not argue. Just how to do it without overisolating the missionary child from the host culture" and preventing his own maturity is quite a different task that "calls for much wisdom and prayer."[12]

Emotional Independence

The umbrella over the previous six contributing factors to the growth and development of the MK's personality in a foreign culture would have to be, in my opinion, the emotional independence that the MK learns early on.

Survey after survey from the parents and the MKs themselves mentioned this element far more than any other result of living in a foreign country.

Because they have had to examine themselves against the contact with two other cultures they have come to know and accept themselves for who they are. Karen's homeroom teacher said that she felt Karen was less apprehensive about entering a new high school this year in the ninth grade than were the other students who had come from the junior high together.—Dale Thorne, Israel.

Going off to boarding school in the seventh grade certainly helped to mature them. They learned to depend on themselves, to travel alone, to meet crises without the physical support of parents.—Pauline (Mrs. Arville E.) Senter, Liberia.

Our sons have become independent and adept in traveling on their own. My sister-in-law wrote that she was amazed when our sixteen-year-old son (Art, Jr.), visiting

her in Tampa, Florida, took a city map and bicycled all
over Tampa. She stated that not one of her sons would
have dared to do such.—Martha (Mrs. A.R.) Haylock,
Dominican Republic.

As one MK freshman coed summed it up, "I have
learned to make friends easily due to my development in
Uruguay, and I have learned to do many things on my
own."

Growing up in another culture shapes and developes
the MK. His personality will be molded by many aspects
from the cultures of which he is a part.

A large part of that personality will be affected by his
relationships with others beyond his immediate family—
fellow MKs, nationals, and his American (and/or British,
German) peers.

My major professor at Southwestern Seminary, John
Drakeford, often reminded us in classes and seminars,
"The process of socialization involves a group which could
be called a microcosm or small world exercising both a
corrective and supportive function for the growing individual."[13]

The microcosm or the MK's group will vary from country to country depending upon circumstances.

Where he is relatively isolated, his group will be cen-
tered around his family.

Where he is one of the very few or the only MK, in the
presence of many national children his age, he will likely
identify and build his group around them.

If he is one of many MKs, for example in a boarding
school for MKs, or there are many American children (or
other nationalities), he will build his world around that
particular group.

Of course, where several options exist, he may choose
to integrate them or choose to identify with only one
group.

Franklin Fowler contrasted the limited peer group of the MK with that of his peer in the United States: "Where the United States child will have several groups, that of his school, his church, his neighborhood, and community, the missionary child will tend to have fewer. If he is in a mission school or boarding school, this may be limited to one group, the missionary children with whom he lives."[14]

Consequently, the third culture MK may be handicapped or have an advantage.[15]

From his personal experiences, Fowler described the third world culture environment as "restrictive and frustrating, even cruel, but most of the time it is thrilling, widening, maturing and learning from several cultures."[16]

Let's look at a variety of possibilities as MKs cope with their environments and build relationships in their world.

MKs, Their Relationships and the Results

Sibling Relationships May Become Stronger

We have examined the idea of the family unit being stronger than its American counterpart in chapter 1. We also saw in this chapter how a culture's view of the sex of a child can have an influence. Put together a family with older boys and a younger girl and add a culture that strongly separates the two, and you get this result.

In our culture boys and girls do not play together, but our daughter was 'allowed' to play soccer with the boys because Philip said it was his ball, and she could play.— Barbara (Mrs. George M.) Workman, Malawi.

Take one MK sister, not a Christian, and add the concern of her sister, a Christian, and you get this strong bond.

Janet prayed with her sister Susan, witnessing her deci-

sion for Christ. With tears streaming down their faces,
they came to tell us the good news.—Martha (Mrs. A. R.)
Haylock, Dominican Republic.

Barriers Between Races Can Be Overcome
Take the MKs, their love for their national peers and
that child, and mix them together: "Our kids have a
chocolate sister. She is one of the family."—Jenny (Mrs.
James D.) Musen, Kenya.

A Spiritual Sensitivity for the Lost
Consider a formative five-year-old, dinner table conversation about unchurched friends, his inquisitive mind,
and you have this scene.

Recently, around the dinner table, some friends were
mentioned in the conversation. They do not attend
church. They also have a five-year-old. Something was
said about how sad it is for them not to be learning about
Jesus. With all the sincerity and determination he could
muster, our five-year-old looked at me and asked, "Daddy, why don't they want to learn about and love Jesus?—
Felix V. Greer, Jr., Liberia.

Compassion for the Less Fortunate
Combine the senses of seeing and hearing in a four-
year-old with the poverty before him and add his financial
resources and concern, and you get this result.

After seeing and hearing of the needs in Korea, our
four-year-old wanted to take his pennies and give one to
each family in our area.—Anthony Stella, Jr., Korea.

Opportunity Early to Learn to Share One's Faith in a
Natural Manner
Take a young MK fluent in English, a Chinese high

school student wanting to learn English, the gospel, and you get this story.

When our son was primary school age, a young Chinese high school student came to our home seeking to practice his English. Our son helped him by showing him the Bible and reading John 3:16 to him.—Mr. and Mrs. Jack Gentry, Taiwan.

Temporary but often difficult Adjustment to Isolation

Combine an adolescent girl, cultural and social limitations, and you have this adjustment.

Our daughter is in early adolescence, and things are sometimes difficult for her. We are fortunate to live on the main highway in the country, so that our entire mission family must come through here to go almost anywhere else. We try to get together every two or three weeks for overnight visits with other MKs. She will be going to boarding school about 1,000 miles away in two years, but, right now, she has a lot of lonely days. Girls in this culture are getting ready to marry at eleven and twelve. They have no time to be a child, and adolescence is something they hardly know. Still, she seems content with her present lot, able to accept it as temporary though somewhat painful.—Delinda (Mrs. Ronald J.) Miller, Malawi.

Ability to Respond to Adversity in a Mature Manner

Picture a young teenage boy having fun, a group of national boys in opposition to him, a concerned father, a national pastor, and you witness this mature insight from that MK.

Our son Wade had made a raft and had taken it to a lake in our residential area to sail. While he was in a narrow part of the lake some boys started throwing stones, and Wade was hit on the cheek by half of a brick. He came home bruised and bleeding. I tried not to show my anger at these boys, so I cleaned Wade up. I felt certain he hadn't provoked the incident as long ago he'd learned to mind his own business and not to respond to teasing or unkind remarks. It seemed the boys had really taken advantage of having him in a narrow place where he couldn't get away. However, we didn't want him to become afraid or distrust the Bengalis, so we asked our national pastor to talk with Wade about the ugly affair. Our pastor came away from their talk smiling. He said, "Wade's fine! He told me there are unkind people everywhere we go, and Bangladesh is no different than anywhere else."—James F. McKinley, Jr., Bangladesh.

Opportunity to Have Experiences and Be Exposed to Circumstances That Can Be Positive and Interesting

For example, what do a female MK, a baby goat and other gifts, plus proposals of marriage have in common?

Our daughter has received unique gifts such as a baby goat. She has been asked for in marriage since she was twelve.—Sharon (Mrs. J. E.) McPherson, Gaza.

Consider the *culta de quince años*, the highly important date in the life of a teenage girl in Mexico, the observance of her fifteenth birthday. According to one article[17] on this event, some people living in small towns take whole pages in the paper to announce the event while another offered his daughter her choice, the party or a trip to Europe. The party is a social occasion and usually a large dance is held as part of the celebration. Many Christians decide to hold the recognition srvice at the church and make it a religious event.

Leland Webb described this possibility in the case of MK Becky Bridges.

When Becky Bridges was fifteen years old, her friends and neighbors were invited to the church where she wore a formal white dress; attendants preceeded her down the church aisle to a platform decorated by baskets of flowers. Long strands of greenery draped the building on either side of the auditorium. After the congregation had sung a hymn, the pastor read 1 Corinthians 13 and preached a 30-minute sermon.

"The message was evangelistic," Mrs. Bridges explained later to a non-Spanish-speaking guest. "A number of our friends and neighbors, some of them Catholics, were present. One said to me afterward, 'That was a beautiful ceremony.' Another said, 'That was interesting. I'd like to talk to you more about it.' "

After the message Becky knelt while her father, who had been seated on the platform, led in prayer. Then everyone crossed a small patio to a room prepared for the reception. A poster proclaiming "15 *primaveras* [springs]" features snapshots of Becky at various ages. Following the Mexican version of "Happy Birthday," Becky blew out the candles on the cake, and everyone lined up for a piece of cake, a tamale or two, and a soft drink.

Webb observed: "A fifteen-year-old MK had reaped one benefit of living in another culture—her own *culta de quince años.*"[18]

Leisuretime, Interests, Hobbies, and Witness

In chapter 3 we saw the influence of the MK's parents upon the MK, how the MKs responded to their parents' work, different ways they became involved, and how some MKs feel led to return to their foreign country as career missionaries themselves.

MKs, like all children, must grow spiritually on their own. They cannot live off the commitment of their parents. Living in another country often gives them some rather unique opportunities to witness.

I asked MKs at an annual MK weekend this question:

"Have your hobbies or your use of leisuretime, special skills, etc., provided you with an opportunity to lead someone to Jesus Christ, and if so could you share it below?"

The responses were varied and most interesting, giving a better understanding of their positions and opportunities. I have placed them into six categories.

1. The knowledge that this is what God wants and the conviction to begin.

One of several MKs responded to the question, "No, this is something I must work on."

MKs are not super Christians just because their parents are missionaries. They are not biblical scholars or theologians because their parents attended and/or graduated from seminary. They also must struggle to grow spiritually.

2. The desire to give back one's talents and capabilities to God for His use.

I find that as a Christian if you use your talents and abilities for God's glory and let Him use you and work through you, then He can work miracles—not only overseas but here in the States.—Jonja Deal, Jordan.

3. The opportunity to use special honors and recognition to witness.

I am very involved in Scouts. I have had the honor to be the American Legion National Scout of the Year in 1979. I have used this as a witness to young boys.—David Gregory, Mexico.

4. Use of the medium of music to witness.

Yes, I love to sing and witness through that medium of music. We would go to churches and schools and present Christ to them through songs and testimony. It was so exciting to see people come to know Him as we know Him. Christ is universal, and it was really special to see that firsthand.—Stephen James, East Asia.

I play the guitar and sing, and as I've sung people have come and talked to me, and opportunity after opportunity has come about. Of course, being a girl also brings attention to which you can turn into a chance to share. I work with kids, and that too is a real neat way to share Christ.—Lorrie G. Horton, Kenya.

5. Witness through the medium of sports.

I used sports as a means of testimony.—Laurence Cole, South Brazil.

I play on the varsity soccer team. So far, two players have come to know Christ.—Steve Beck, Indonesia.

Our oldest son loves motorcycle rides to the 'bush.' It calls attention and conversations when he asks directions which opens doors for a return visit.—Kay (Mrs. Paul) Eaton, Tanzania.

Their interest in music and sports has resulted in their making many friends and influencing some of them toward Christ and church attendance. Gary, Junior Golf Champ of Zambia in 1976, made friends with golfers all over Zambia and witnessed to many. Randy and Bruce's soccer heroics gained many friends and admirers.—Joy (Mrs. Fred M.) Allen, Zambia.

Bicycling has helped John find friends and develop relationships which later gave opportunities for witnessing.—Mildred (Mrs. Victor R.) Watts, Bophuthatswana.

6. Witness through every means possible.

I have been able to *share* Jesus with people on the Taiwan trains.—Grace Morris, Taiwan.

Some of us MKs organized prayer meetings. At school and at camp young people were led to Christ through our Christian love.—Steve Baker, Israel.

Our oldest is quite good at translating puppet plays, and

our young people use extensively the puppet ministry to witness both in church and in the city plazas.—Marjorie (Mrs. Robert D.) Worley, Spain.

I love to listen to people and counsel with people. I feel this is a real need and something being an MK has helped to develop in me. It has been used of God.—Brigitte Atnip, Rhodesia.

Our children took horseback-riding lessons and our whole family had opportunities to show our Christian lifestyle and express verbally and in acts of concern our Christian testimony. Several friends were invited and attended our church. Through this 'hobby' we met many influential people, businessmen, etc., whom we never would have met otherwise.—Ellen (Mrs. Phil) Overton, Barbados, West Indies.

Our younger daughter has given several acts with her ventriloquist doll.—Annette (Mrs. Robert) Crockett, Argentina.

Don't Pity the MK

Growing up in another culture is a unique experience. It isn't the same as growing up in the United States. Each country brings its own characteristics peculiar to that culture. They are neither all bad, nor all good, but God has given the MK the opportunity to become the person He wants him to be within that culture. Some MKs will adapt easily, and others will not adapt as well. Parents will make mistakes in trying to make the best decisions, some very painful. But don't pity the MK.

Frank Means, former Board secretary for South America, made a statement concerning missionaries which applies equally to their children. "Missionaries are surprisingly resourceful in adjusting to the demands made upon them by emergencies and crises of one kind or another."

MKs come through their unique experiences, and the vast majority are glad they had that opportunity to live and grow up overseas. Just ask them about it!

Notes

1. Lawrence K. Frank, "Cultural Control and Physiological Autonomy," in *Personality in Nature, Society, and Culture*, eds. Clyde Kluckhohn, Henry A. Murray, and David M. Schneider (New York: Alfred A. Knopf, 1967), pp. 119-22.

2. Delmer R. Guyner, "A Study of Relationships Between Selected Personality Factors and Personal Adjustment of Overseas Personnel," Ed. D. dissertation, North Texas State University, 1975, p. 17.

3. Franklin T. Fowler to William C. Viser, 2 Nov. 1981.

4. Ibid.

5. Wendell M. Swenson, John S. Pearson, and David Osborne, *An MMPI Source Book* (Minneapolis: University of Minnesota Press, 1973), p. 3.

6. Frank S. Freeman, *Theory and Practice of Psychological Testing*, 3rd ed. (New York: Holt, Rinehart, and Winston, 1962), p. 562.

7. William C. Bier, "A Modified Form of the Minnesota Multiphasic Personality Inventory for Religious Personnel," *Theological Education* 7 (1971), p. 3.

8. William C. Viser, "A Psychological Profile of Missionary Children in College and the Relationship of Intense Group Therapy to Weekly Group Therapy in the Treatment of Personality Problems as Reflected by the Minnesota Multiphasic Personality Inventory," Ed. D. dissertation, Southwestern Baptist Theological Seminary, 1978, pp. 78-92.

9. Ray F. Davis, "A Look at the Third Culture Child," *Japan Christian Quarterly* 42 (Spring 1976), p. 66.

10. Jeannine Willmon, "An MK Comes Home," *The Commission*, Aug. 1971, p. 23.

11. Ibid., p. 23.

12. Franklin Fowler, "The Third World Culture of the MK," *The Commission*, Dec. 1970, pp. 2-3.

13. John W. Drakeford, *Integrity Therapy* (Nashville:Broadman Press, 1967), p. 10.

14. Fowler, "The Third World Culture of the MK," p. 1.

15. "Question of the Week," *Japan Times*, 5 Sept. 1976.

16. Fowler, "The Third World Culture of the MK," p. 3.

17. Leland Webb, "Ceremony at 15," *The Commission*, Aug. 1971, p. 21.

18. Ibid., p. 21.

5
The Coming Home Shock: An MK Returns to the United States

Take a long look around you. You will not have to look far to find an MK. They come in all ages and classifications. Some are babies, others are elementary schoolchildren. They are teenagers, college students, single or married adults. Some of them will be very easy for you to get to know and others will not open up quite so easily, but they are well worth the effort to establish a relationship.

There is one thing they all have in common in this chapter—the United States. All MKs at one time—and usually several times—will come back to the United States, and what will be their experience? For some it will be only a time of waiting until the furlough is over, and they can get back to "the field"; for some it will be a time filled with many pleasant and precious memories. For others it will be a mixture of good and bad experiences. If I might be so bold, I offer the opinion that the positiveness or negativeness of the furlough experience for the MK will depend on these factors:

1. The age of the MK,
2. How his parents have or have not prepared him,
3. His overseas experience,
4. The personality of the MK,
5. That knowledgeable pastor and/or church staff member, and, last but not least, YOU! That's right. I hope that you will hold on to the insights from the previous chapters

and consider those I will be sharing with you in this chapter. They could well be the door to a beautiful relationship with some beautiful people.

Let's begin by looking at misconceptions about missionary children. I have chosen to call this

Eleven Myths About MKs

1. MKs feel they have "given up much" because their parents are missionaries. To think this is understandable but, fortunately, is not true when you talk with most MKs.

Yes, they do face adjustments that their peers in the US do not, and their US peers or adults really have no basis from which to understand such adjustments except to conclude that anytime one lives beyond the borders of the United States, he has made a great sacrifice.

While on furlough in 1982-1983, I was speaking to a group of GAs. A ten-year-old girl came up to me afterwards and questioned me at length about the dress of Brazilian young people and the lack of American brands to buy in Brazil. She finally exclaimed, "Boy, I don't think I could give up my designer shirts and jeans!"

In another state I had the joy of talking to a group of young people who wanted to know more about "life in general" in Brazil. "Do you have cable television?" "No," I responded. I could tell he was really having a hard time understanding this foreign country where I had served for three and one-half years. He tried one more time and said, "Well, surely they have video games?" When I responded that they did not have anything like that, he said, in exasperation, "What's the matter with those people. Are they crazy or something?" He just could not imagine that anything so "important" would not exist in another country.

One teenager, Donny Lockerbie, had the opportunity to travel around the world. Prior to his trip to mission stations throughout Asia, parts of Africa, and the Middle East he had what he called his "Dr. Livingston I presume" impression of missions [a missionary wearing a pith helmet, safari suit, driving a Land Rover, and preaching to the accompaniment of beating drums and boiling cannibal pots]. What he discovered totally changed his perspective. Concerning the "giving up much" myth he said: "These kids are happy to be living abroad. They aren't pining away for Grandma's apple pie, even though it's been four years since they tasted it. They're not even homesick for the youth fellowship at First Baptist Church. They have their friends, their good times, especially those who are in schools like Christian Academy in Japan, Morrison Academy in Taiwan, Kodaikonal School in India, Rift Valley Academy in Kenya and Good Shepherd School in Ethiopia. Sure, sometimes they talk about how good a *real* hamburger would taste, but a lot of kids enjoy national foods even better than Yankee pot roast."[1]

Mary Ann Ward wrote that in spite of the difficulties that MKs encounter, they feel they are "privileged" and resent the question, "What have you given up because your parents were missionaries?"[2]

According to Lynn Moss, a student from Zambia, "We have to keep explaining that we don't give up anything. I've gained so much—more than I would have in the States."[3]

I believe Lynn speaks for a majority of MKs.

2. The MK family "has it all together."

Missionary families are subject to challenges and stresses like every other American family. Just because they are missionaries does not mean that they do not face difficult circumstances or that everything is always on "an even keel."

In an article on how to help the missionary on furlough the writer wrote:

The church of which the missionary family becomes a part during furlough can treat the missionaries as real people with the same problems, hurts, and joys as any other family. Nobody enjoys being treated as a "revered" person, put on a pedestal, and not able to enjoy normal life. Even missionaries sometimes make mistakes, fail to correct the children properly, even lose their tempers! The church can love them and support them and help them as they would another member.[4]

3. MKs consider the US "home" and cannot wait for furloughs to come.

Let's divide this section into two parts which will enable us to "defuse" this myth more clearly.

First, a distinction needs to be made between *home* and *homeland.*

"Although 'home' is where their parents are on the field, the 'homeland' for MKs is still the United States," said the late Rogers M. Smith, special assistant to the president at the Foreign Mission Board.[5]

Second, even though the MK has this "homeland concept" of the United States in mind, the thought of it in reality can be difficult.

MK Charlene Martin of Tanzania stated, "I thought I might have to spend the rest of my life living in the United States and it frightened me to death."[6]

Why the fear? It might be traced to a totally different culture in which they have grown up. It might be traced to a high degree of mobility where the family has moved frequently. Perhaps the MK is inclined toward the shy side. Remember, this is a time when peer acceptance is difficult enough for a US teenager, much less a teenager from another country trying to fit into a peer culture that likely dresses differently, talks differently, and has a subculture of his own. Add these together, and it is small wonder some MKs feel overwhelmed by it all.

In spite of it all, MKs want and need the same security that all of us desire. Miss Martin continued:

"We crave security because we've moved around so much. . . . We crave a place to call home."[7]

Initially, the United States does not always offer that sense of security so that MKs consider it home.

But, you might ask, doesn't the furlough experience that MKs go through several times help them adjust? It may, and it may not.

Furlough is intended to be a time of rest and recuperation, of sharing God's blessings, and exciting people to give of themselves and make financial commitments to mission work, of educating people concerning missions, and making purchases of clothing and other items for the next term of service.

Missionaries are required to accept invitations to participate in world missions conferences or camps, depending on how long their furlough lasts and they do this gladly. However, this can become part of the problem, since some accept too many invitations.

One colleague told me of permitting his calendar to fill too rapidly. He was gone almost all the time until his wife told him of an incident at a restaurant with their two young sons. It seems as if the mother was eating dinner alone with the two boys during one of their father's frequent trips out of town when the youngest one tapped his mother on the arm and said, "Mother, look at that man over there. Isn't that Daddy?" It wasn't, but his calendar shaped up considerably shortly after that.

One writer put it in these words:

Where some might think the MKs looked forward to furlough times to be "home" in the U.S. and with family, furlough is actually a difficult period. Parents are "Lottie Mooning," raising money for the annual foreign missions offering. "Friends" have grown up with different values and relatives are strangers. Home—be it in Africa, South America or Asia—is still where your friends are and where you pour out your life.[8]

4. MKs return to the United States on furlough and just "slip right into place."

This is definitely a myth. If you have ever traveled out of the United States or been away from your hometown for a significant period of time, you have returned to find some changes or discover something that happened in your absence.

Multiply that by four years, and you might get the idea.

When we returned from Brazil on furlough in June 1982, we suddenly discovered a world of video games. They were everywhere and very much a part of children's and teenagers' vocabulary. TV cable companies and "dishes" in backyards to receive signals from satellites were commonplace to the average American but not to us. A lot can and does happen in four years, and it takes time before you begin to feel "at home" with all the changes.

There is also the matter of *where* you furlough. It may be close to an MK's ill grandparents on one furlough or close to elderly grandparents on another furlough. It may be to permit Dad or Mom to do further study. It may be to work with a state convention on another furlough. The possibility that the MK's furlough will be in the same place twice is not very likely.

When I surveyed my missionary colleagues of South Brazil, I asked for a yes or no response to: "I generally furlough in the same location each time I return to the US."

Fifty percent did, and 50 percent did not. Significantly enough, of the 50 percent who did, the feeling was unanimous that it was a positive factor in the adjustment of the child. Of the 50 percent responding no, 67 percent felt it would be beneficial to furlough in the same location.

When asked about what regrets she had about her upbringing, one MK responded:

"I wish my family's home leaves or furloughs could have been in one place in the U.S. We went back three times and lived in three different places. I can't really say or feel I'm from anywhere in the States."[9]

Truman Smith addressed this matter:

"Living in the same location in the U.S. on more than one furlough gives an MK an opportunity to develop friendships that could last into the college years. At least there is someone whom he would know that he could look up if he chose to do so."[10]

I tend to agree. There are exceptions, and I have heard some MKs comment favorably about the varied and exciting opportunities that have been afforded them by always furloughing in a different place. However, I believe that "a little permanency" in this area could go a long way in helping the MK feel secure.

5. MKs love to be the center of attention.

After talking "teenager to teenager" to MKs he visited around the world, Donny Lockerbie put together a composite picture of what happens to many MKs as they become the center of attention, for example, in a church.

As soon as they arrive, the Sunday School superintendent grabs them and yanks each off to some class where the teacher decides to give up the fight to keep attention by interviewing the newly arrived MK. The teacher asks a lot of "spiritual" questions, like "What's the status of the indigenous church in Nagaland?" and the fifteen-year-old is supposed to know! Right away he feels on display.

Some MKs will be very much involved in their parents' work and will *want* to share about it. Others will not be so deeply involved, and they will choose not to share.

All of us are called to be missionaries. Matthew 28:19-20 leaves no room for doubt in this matter. The parents of the MK are *called* to be vocational missionaries on a foreign field. It is their *calling*, their *career*, and they are *supported financially* to do that work and it alone. The MK becomes part of that by virtue of his being a son or daughter. Unfortunately, some confuse this position, and because he is an MK they want to consider him as a "little missionary" and put him in the "spotlight." Many MKs are not comfortable with such attention.

6. All MKs are alike.

This misconception is easy to hold.

MKs understand MKs far more than anyone outside of that category. It is not surprising that MKs should develop such a close relationship with one another. Ruth Fowler observed that MKs have something pretty special among them, above and beyond the close friendships that many high school classmates develop. In almost every respect they shared a certain kinship which compares to a family feeling.[11]

But what family member is exactly like another? Even in the same family they can show drastically different personalities, and so do MKs.

Not every MK is musically talented. Some MKs will rebel to the full extent possible—no different from the PK (preacher's kid), deacon's kid, or the average layperson's kid.

Even the title *MK* presents subtle problems.

One felt you are an MK first and a person second.[12]

D. Bruce Lockerbie elaborated that it is not so much the term as it is the associations that go with it. A mentality that readily lumps together individual persons and makes them into "MKs"—packaged entities presumably typed, classified, and cataloged—is what disturbs so many. It ignores the person and looks instead at the supposed class.[13]

Marjorie Collins pursued the thought a step further by maintaining that missionary children should be allowed to live a normal, happy life no different from other children and should not be made to feel that they must abide by altogether different principles.[14]

MKs are growing people, and each one grows in his own unique manner.

7. MKs are "super Christians."

This is a stereotype that is often held by many. It will also apply to the missionary parent as well.

As an MK from Brazil said, "Missionaries aren't superhumans. They're just like everyone else."[15]

Another added, "People don't understand that MKs have needs too,"[16] while another stated, "People also assume MKs are real nice kids. Not all of us are."[17]

Sometimes the foreign field itself can make spiritual growth somewhat difficult for the MK, especially where the language is extremely difficult to master. Consider what these two MKs have to share concerning this, first the girl and then the boy:

"I feel different in my national church than in an American church. I know that much for sure! I don't feel as close to the Lord in the services, as when the service is in English."

The boy responded, "Many opportunities to witness are lost because of not knowing the language well enough and being afraid that you will scare him away instead of getting him to come to church and accept Christ. In America I usually enjoy going to church and listening to the sermons. But when the sermon is in the native language, I often would rather not go because I have to think hard to translate what the preacher is saying."

Let's pursue this line of thought along a little different line in the next myth.

8. MKs are "biblical scholars."

Some assume that because the MK's parents are missionaries who have studied at a seminary, the MK will also be extremely knowledgeable about the Bible.

The MK must make his own spiritual pilgrimage like his parents before him. As the late Catherine Marshall put it, "God has no grandsons."[18] The MK cannot borrow from his parents. If he is to know the Bible, he must discover it for himself.

Circumstances peculiar to each MK can make Bible study a different experience for the MK in contrast to his American peers.

First, he will likely not enjoy the highly developed educational program that stateside churches enjoy with well defined curriculum and trained teachers to present the material and related learning activities.

Second, he will not have the benefit of a highly organized youth program with regular times of Bible study, discipleship training, and a host of other stimulating aids to Bible study.

The fact of the matter is, he may be involved in teaching. Here is one MK's experience.

"Our Africans weren't quick to learn, and evidently we went over and over the same things. I know well the stories of Jesus, but who was Balaam and Barak?"[19] Her conclusion was that MKs are not always knowledgeable about the Bible.

9. MKs want "special privileges."

I believe what MKs want more than anything else is simply to be accepted and regarded as a person of worth.

He neither wants to be "pitied," nor to be elevated to "sainthood status."

Many will want to do things for him, and this is usually very much appreciated. As one MK shared with me, "I appreciate anything anyone gives me. I have enjoyed this."

However, "going out and looking" for special privileges would only tend to further separate and isolate him from the normal way she wants to be regarded.

10. MKs are different.

Consider the following children's poem and comments:

> Little Indian, Sioux or Crow,
> Little frosty Eskimo,
> Little Turk or Japanee,
> Oh! don't you wish that you were me?
> ....
> You have curious things to eat,
> I am fed on proper meat;
> You must dwell beyond the foam,
> But I am safe and live at home.

Written almost one hundred years ago, Robert Louis Stevenson's verse for children seems today quaintly old-fashioned. But is it really? While expressing such thoughts now would generally be considered tasteless, it remains that children brought up in one culture tend to view the others as different and sometimes inferior.[20]

Bill Hatton, an MK from South Brazil, described how he believes people in the US see him: "They view me as coming from a disadvantaged corner of the world. How could I tell them that the city of Rio de Janeiro, a metropolis of 6.5 million people and a major cultural and economic center of the Western Hemisphere, is an area far superior to many places in the United States? It's frustrating for people to think you're from the jungle, when you've come from a larger urban area than most Southern Baptists live in."[21]

That "different tag" is often placed on the MK just by mention of where he is from.

One MK said, "I dread being asked that. It sets me apart."[22] Another related, "I feel rather strange when people ask me where I am from,' she added. 'I answer "Spain," and they respond, "Oh!' "[23] Another shared that when her roommate discovered that she was an MK from Spain the roommate expected someone weird.[24]

Carrying that "different category" a step further into the stereotyped view of MKs and their parents, an African MK related, "Most people think my parents live in a little grass hut without running water and go around stalking the bush country looking for people to convert."[25]

11. MKs are "problem kids." Some do have their difficulties but no more so than any other young person.

In fact, carried to its extremes, an in-depth study by sociologist Dr. Ruth Hill Useem and several scholars at Michigan State University led to the conclusion that TCKs (third culture kids) have fewer psychiatric problems than young people from similar backgrounds in the US.[26]

Lane feels, and rightly so, that "the problem MK gets enough attention as it is."[27]

Let me conclude this section with an insight from a young person in the US about his peers from other countries.

"I want to ask, on behalf of my new friends, that we treat MKs like ordinary kids. One year is so short when trying to make adjustments to find your way in a new school. We've got to be more sensitive to their obvious needs for personal identity."[28]

So be it!

Eleven Generalizations About MKs

As we lay to rest the myths about MKs, we have a better basis for our coming to know them and establish meaningful friendships. Now I want to share with you eleven more findings from Dr. Ruth Useem's research.[29] Concerning MKs she stated, "Speaking personally, it does seem that many of these generalizations can more safely be made about children with long term experience in a single overseas location (notably missionary children)." These findings suggest that third culture children:

1. Are more intimately related to and dependent upon the family than would be true in the United States. Parents play a more potent role in the socialization of their children. In a research project carried out among TCKs in Manila, 90 percent of the respondents listed "parents" when asked to identify their best friends.

2. Appear more sophisticated than the average in relations with adults but may be relatively inexperienced and insecure in peer group relations, particularly with members of the opposite sex.

3. Do not make friends easily but depend on one or two very close friends.

4. Are self-directed, self-disciplined, subdued on the surface but likely to think deeply and seriously about both personal and community concerns.

5. Are good observers (they "are comparative from the word go").

6. Are gaining in measured intellectual performance at the same time that general test scores in the US are going down.

7. Do a great deal of reading—frequently in adult materials—and are more likely to enjoy writing than peers in the US. Their often long letters constitute an

example of a nearly extinct skill among their contemporaries at home.

8. Are more likely to be accomplished to some degree in the field of music.

9. Are more conservative in values than their peers in the US.

10. Take academic work seriously and are frequently overachievers. (Dr. Useem notes, however, that life is not at all easy for the small percentage with serious academic or personal problems. She notes that the third culture typically does not provide the services for those with problems, adult or child, which have come to be accepted as standard in the home culture.)

11. Lack models in the twenty-to twenty-five-year-old age group.

As we have seen, the foreign culture will play a major role in the formation of that personality.

An MK from Japan stated: "Growing up here has influenced my personality." She smiled. "I think I've taken on some of the characteristics of the Japanese. I felt more reserved than the others in college. I worried about offending people. I was usually quiet, kind of observing. I knew I was different, but I didn't want to make a big point of it."[30]

One's self-image is certainly not to be taken lightly. Every person has to come to grips with it; the MK is no exception. Their experiences in the United States will play a role in that image.

MK Mary Carpenter of Indonesia shared, "I didn't realize how different I was until junior high. . . . I didn't have an identity problem until we got back to the United States. In Indonesia, I thought we had everything. We ran around barefoot and with few clothes. But here we looked like little beggars."[31]

Reflecting on her experiences, MK Janene Weller related. "I looked like an American and was expected to know how to act, to know the lingo, what's cool and what's gross. But I had questions about simple things those who grew up in America never have to think about. Is it okay to ask to use someone's fingernail clippers or is that like asking to use his toothbrush? Do you pay for water?"[32]

Another said, "So many things I don't know. Like not knowing how to use a pay telephone or keep a bowling score or work an automatic washing machine. And how embarrassing to go shopping. I never know if I have enough money or not because of silly taxes. Why don't they just put the real price on things and be done with it? People have a big laugh and explain, 'Look, she's from Africa. She doesn't know any better.' or 'Hey, kids, she's lived in France and doesn't even know what French kissing is! Ha, ha.'"[33]

Adjustment for the elementary school age MK is not the problem that it is for the teenage MK.

Dr. Sidney Frenkel, director of computer support for military psychiatry at Walter Reed Hospital in Washington, DC, said, "In elementary school there is little problem with traveling about, and in pre-school no problem. But being uprooted in the high school years is difficult. They're growing rapidly and react strongly to everything."[34]

"This judgment is generally shared by counselors and educators familiar with the problem. When TCKs return to the states they are three or four years socially retarded according to Dr. Gordon Parsons, regional officer in the state department and the biggest problem they face is the feeling of not belonging."[35]

One MK expressed the feeling in this statement, "I find myself looking like two hundred million other Americans but I feel different and don't know their habits, customs, and expectations."[36]

Attending an unfamiliar high school during furlough can be a traumatic experience. The MK is thrown into a school where everyone knows each other already. Cliques are already formed, and many high school students don't bother to get to know someone who will stay only one year.

One MK described her first encounter with her peers: "At first everyone gathered around me wanting to know about the country where I live. After that I never saw them again."

A mother once said that her teenage daughter sat at home after school waiting for the phone to ring.

Every MK does not have the same problem as these and will fit in easier. He must commit himself to wanting relationships with his peers, but time is working against him as his parent's furlough will only last so long, and he is also trying to come to grips with a culture that he does not totally understand at an age where to not know the right things to say and do can create even greater isolation.

"It's as if they have come to a foreign land and yet are not foreigners—like aliens, but not having the advantage of being alien. Everyone expects them to know the latest college idiom—and they don't. They feel 'out of it,' " said Dr. Jay Chambers, director of the Center for Psychological Services at the College of William and Mary.[37]

To feel "out of it" is devastating at an age when peer group acceptance means everything. And most vulnerable to the trials of transience are the thirteen-to eighteen-year-olds whose confidence and popularity hinge on being "hip" to the current jargon and styles.[38]

"Shyness is mistaken for snobbishness, hesitation for unwillingness and ignorance for lack of interest."[39]

An MK from Japan put it in this perspective: "Now my parents realize they should have taught me more about United States history and customs. When my college friends used to talk about politics or football, I just kept my mouth closed."[40] The same would hold true for the teenage MK not in college.

Lockerbie drew the following conclusion:

> Is it any wonder that so many of these teenagers feel lost? Until I met some of them on their home turf, I'd always thought that MKs were just naturally 'out of it.' Now I think I understand their sense of alienation a little better. I'm not surprised they didn't know about Watergate or who won the Super Bowl. I understand why they didn't know that James Taylor and Carly Simon are married. Nobody bothers to tell them things like this. We just ask questions about how many heathen are being saved and expect them to be authorities.[41]

MKs may have to catch up on jargon, clothes, music, television, movies, and leisuretime fads, but perhaps the most difficult area is dating.

You need only live overseas to realize that dating as it is known in the MK's country is usually drastically different from what it is in the United States, different in terms of what you expect from the relationship, what you do, where you go, how you get there, and other areas. Some of the differences will be identified as MKs relate dating customs in their particular countries. First, let's look at some comments concerning dating in general.

Dating is a normal custom in the United States. Society, and particularly the advertising media, has placed more and more emphasis on the boy-girl relationship at an early age. We have only to witness the success of certain movies and observe commercials on television to be convinced. While completing work on my Doctor of Education degree, I read research describing some schools with formals where boys and girls ten years of age and younger were dressing in tuxedos and formals. The girls went to beauty shops to have their hair done for the dance! No wonder child psychologist David Elkind in his book *The Hurried Child* wrote, "The concept of children, so vital to the traditional American way of life, is threatened with extinction in the society we have created."[42]

This emphasis, subliminal or conscious, which bombards children in the US tends to create the environment which MKs face while on furlough. Some MKs have no problems at all adjusting; others do. For many, their initial attempts to cope with dating will not be easy emotionally.

Some teenagers who come to the US have not dated before or have dated under more limited circumstances.

When I asked MKs the question "Could you comment on how dating customs in your country differ from those of the US and how this can have an effect on the MK?" one responded jokingly, "What's dating? Seriously, in Jordan dates were chaperoned after a liaison set it up."

One male MK from Ecuador confirmed this from personal experience, "I was chaperoned on my first three dates."

"The Chinese thought I was too young to date at age seventeen. They just don't date very much in the teen years. I lived at an American school, however, so I did date. Dating at my school was considered 'serious' after one or two dates."

"In Indonesia, we don't date much as such. We have lots of girl-guy (relationships) as friends and should it develop into something more, then they go together. It is healthy (the whole concept) because we start out as friends."

A missionary parent shared, "In some areas where standards of morality are low, missionary parents do not want their children to date freely."[43]

One college freshman shared, "I never dated at all and wasn't even around the opposite sex much, with the exception of my father and brothers, until junior high."

Dating in another country can be described more clearly.

"[In] Argentina where girls seldom date over two or three guys . . . it is often the case that once you start going steady you plan to marry each other in the future. This can be very disadvantageous for an MK who is used to dating around because this often causes anger in the girl's parents because they think their daughter's feelings are being played with."

"Dating in Brazil is very strict. You can only date one girl and then you date her for a *very* long time. This has caused me to be more choosy of whom I date."

"In Malaysia, where I grew up, kids are encouraged to 'keep your mind on your studies.' *Nobody* had cars at 16 or 18! Most MKs went out with guys in the schools, sometimes other MKs . . . we didn't date much. I didn't until I was 15, then only at school functions. MK girls rarely dated local boys."

Dating may be defined more in terms of groups of teenagers doing things together as these comments indicate:

"Most of the dating at my school [in Korea] was a group type of dating where everyone went just because they enjoyed each other's company and not because they wanted to start a serious relationship. I think this type of dating is good because it gives the individual a better insight into group relationships, and it helps the individual in relating to other people in a group situation."

"In Japan, or rather the foreign community that I was involved in, [we] did not have much dating. You either were 'going steady' with someone, went out in groups, or did not date at all."

"In Chile, dating does not occur. In most cities young people have a certain street or "plaza" where they get together and meet people their age."

What you do on a date may not hold the wide variety of possibilities that dating in the States does.

"There was no social life in Malawi, and so if you took a girl out you were on your own with only one theater in the city . . . very boring."

The matter of physical closeness and affection may also play a big role in the MK's adjustment to an American system that expresses affection with few restraints.

"In Nigeria when you hold hands, you're having 'sex.' "

Also from an MK with her background in Nigeria, "People of the opposite sex were never seen touching in public, except for the well educated and at night. We had to be really careful in our relationships. I think we still are."

Another MK shared how this affected her, "I feel very sheltered and innocent. Here [US] everybody seems to know everything [about dating]. There is great freedom here in expressing affection on dates. I'm not used to guys coming up and putting their arms around me. I don't know how to react."

When one has such limited experience and/or a totally different cultural idea of dating, one would expect to approach dating in the US on a less than confident basis.

One MK summed it up: "It makes dating in the US an awesome, somewhat fearful prospect."

An MK in college shared his experience with homecoming activities:

"When it came around, I never had dated a girl, and I didn't have the faintest idea what to do. I didn't know what a corsage was. I had to run upstairs to my friends [in the dormitory] and say, hey, listen, what do you guys do during homecoming? I need to ask her to the game. What do you wear, and what do you do? It was slightly embarrassing."

Fortunate is the MK who is familiar with the American system in his mission country as an MK from Liberia stat-

ed, "Dating customs are basically the same since Liberia
has a lot of influence from the US."

"There seem to be two extreme reactions to these unfamiliar cultural situations," according to Franklin Fowler. "Some symbolically lock themselves in the closet in
panic and others take a 'let's try it all' attitude with resulting personal guilt and perhaps deception."[44]

Laura Lane asked the question of college age MKs, "Do
you feel like you have had a more difficult time in dating
than the average college student?" Sixteen percent responded yes, while 68 percent responded no, and 16 percent were unsure.

Two matters bear repeating with reference to what I
have been discussing in this section. First, the personality
of the MK will largely determine how he responds to
those unfamiliar situations, regardless of what they might
be. Second, how much or how little his parents have prepared him can make a significant contribution. Let's look
at this for a moment.

Guidance for Dating

Missionary Parents
Our youngest was somewhat shy, so we tried to emphasize that to have friends you must be friendly! It worked;
he came out of his shell and discovered girls.—Pat (Mrs.
G. Kenneth) Varner, Taiwan.

"I should have, but in the hurry and 'business' I didn't
think to prepare them. Their constant contact with
Americans in Mexico helped."

"We could not prepare them for the racial problems
they were to meet on the school grounds of our hometown school during integration activities of the 60s."

"We talked with them in detail as our plans unfolded,
including their schooling situation. We talked about the

good times, opportunities we would have, and about our relatives. Our children are so happy here they don't want to go on furlough."

At different ages different things were done. American money and values, pictures of the home we were going to, American magazines with current styles in clothing, use of American idioms, and slang were also covered.—Wanda (Mrs. Herbert C.) Edminster, Bophuthatswana.

Yes, we had to prepare them for the adjustment to vastly larger schools, to the discipline of time concerning TV watching, to the reestablishing of relationships with grandparents, uncles, aunts, and cousins. It definitely was needed and hopefully was helpful.—Sherry (Mrs. Robert W.) Sims, Ghana.

Teaching them English, celebrating US holidays such as Thanksgiving and the Fourth of July, even though these are regular work days in Argentina, keeping them in touch with what the US flag looks like as well as teaching them the national anthem.—Clara (Mrs. Barney R.) Hutson, Argentina.

Church Staff Member

As I read through the survey forms returned to me by missionaries throughout the world, I was amazed at how many mentioned that regular contact was maintained with them by the pastor of a church or some other member of the staff. This contact was appreciated by many.

Churches usually know well in advance when a missionary family is to come and stay with them. If there is an emergency of some type, that time might be shortened drastically.

All missionaries want a good experience on furlough for themselves and for their children. The more you know about the missionary family, the better that experience can be.

For example, a letter to the parents prior to their departure to ask them for information about each family member would be helpful. As a missionary parent, I would appreciate this request especially if there were any aspects of my son's or daughter's personality that would be helpful for the church staff to know (shy and withdrawn? little experience with the opposite sex? academic difficulties? athletically minded? musically talented?). Parents might determine if their children want to share about the work in the country rather than put them in an awkward situation in a church group.

MKs are proud of their heritage and are glad to be MKs, but they also want to be treated like ordinary people. The less they are identified as "MKs," and the sooner they fit in as "one of the teenagers" the better everything will be. The last thing they want is to be "put up on a pedestal." This concern was repeated again and again by parents and MKs alike.

If the church staff is multistaff, then responsibilities should be shared by those whose areas the MKs are in.

Not to be forgotten would be those who will be teachers in the Sunday School, choir, Church Training, and various youth positions. A word to them concerning these areas could prevent an uncomfortable situation.

Let me be a little more specific for the minister of youth. I was privileged to be a youth minister for ten years in four churches in Tennessee, Arkansas, and Texas. I had contact with MKs in the last two churches, and I wish I had known then what I know now. I made my share of mistakes!

Youth ministries are extensive and filled with many worthwhile activities. Few, if any, MKs will come into your program from a similar one on the field. Let me make some suggestions:

1. Find out in advance as much as you can about the

MKs who will be in your age responsibility. Especially find out if there are any problem areas, so that you can anticipate them.

2. Write the MK a letter in advance and share your joy that God led him and his family to your church. Share with him some of the coming activities that he *may* want to participate in.

3. Be prepared to assist them financially with the activities. Obviously, this assistance should be offered in a tactful manner.

4. Ask some of your youth to "adopt" that MK while he is home on furlough. They would be responsible for introducing him to other youth, being sure that he had transportation to various events and was made to feel a part of the group. It could be a help if they wrote to the MK as well.

5. Be patient with the MK and do not push too far too fast.

6. Offer to be of help in any way possible. Some MKs told me that it would have been a great help to have someone to talk to in confidence.

7. If the MK has talents, put them to use if he is willing.

8. Give him opportunities to share about his country and, if he wants to, about the work overseas. Some will want to while others will not.

9. Keep the relationship you and the youth group have with him permanent. Remember him in your prayers as a group and ask him to remember you and the youth group in his prayers.

10. Keep in touch with him through the mail. Encourage others to write him as well. You might give each youth a card and give them a specified length of time to write, collect them, and mail them to the MK. Try to remember his birthday and some holidays.

11. Send him a cassette tape of a youth service or youth

choir concerts, youth literature, good books, and/or a magazine subscription.

12. You might even want to fix a care package of stateside items and send it to him.

Two cautions about sending items through the mail:

First, determine that he would like to receive things by mail. Some have said they "love" the care packages they receive, but others may not.

Second, determine what the policy is in his country regarding packages and their contents. The customs charges may prohibit your sending packages.

Many of these suggestions would be applicable in drawing any young person into the youth group; and this is how MKs want to be regarded, just like any other young person.

And YOU, the Church Member

Consider these comments from parents and MKs as they share what has been a blessing to them in past furloughs and what has not been of value. Churches sincerely love their missionaries and want to show it, and missionaries love doing what God has called them to do and those who give to make it possible. A good furlough experience will prove to be a great blessing for all concerned.

Our first furlough was with the First Baptist Church of Texarkana, Texas. It was a positive experience for us. We had a nice clean apartment with plenty of room for a seven-year-old boy to play outside. Our cupboards were overflowing with food. A family in the church gave us free use of one of their cars for the year we were home. We were invited to speak, but they gave us an opportunity to catch our breath first. We became involved in numerous facets of church life, but we were never pressured or asked to do more. We were given a huge baby shower when our daughter Lauren was born. Mothers asked if

Ryan could come over and play or spend the night with
their sons. We were invited into homes for dinner and
supported financially by the church and through gifts of
different individuals far more than we deserved, and a
reception was held on the night we joined and again on
our last Sunday there. They even named a round table
(women's group) after us. We felt genuinely loved, and
that is the key to it all. Let's look at seven ways of showing
love to MKs.

Seven Ways to Show Love to MKs

Love Through Understanding the MK's Desire to Relate to Others

Many churches try to help MKs in many ways which I
really appreciate. Many times though, they put us up on
a pedestal which is often hard to live up to. This makes it
hard for us to relate to others, especially our own peers,
for they see how the church treats us.—An MK from
Malaysia.

We have had people come up to our daughter saying,
"So you're a real live MK."—A missionary mother.

Love Through Acceptance of the MK as a Person

They could accept us as we are and not try to change
us, analyze or understand us. There is no way they can
completely understand. Many churches try to force us on
their youth groups. That makes the youth resent us more
many times.—An MK from East Asia.

Treat MKs as normal people, not superholy kids that
must be looked on with awe. MKs are people too! Churches should be friendly but not pushy. They should not expect the MK to become a part of their lives immediately.
Adjustment is often difficult.—An MK from Jordan.

The church was very mission minded and had many

mission activities which our children participated in with great enthusiasm. This particularly helped our oldest child to know what an MK is and to know what a missionary is. She was just three and one-half when we came to Hong Kong, so her whole life was Hong Kong, missionaries, and being an MK. She didn't know she was any different from any other little girl in the States. When she found out that GAs study about missionaries and are interested in MKs, it gave her a very positive self-image and a new awareness of who she is and what her parents do.— Charlotte (Mrs. Larry D.) Phillips, Hong Kong.

Don't keep pointing out that MKs are MKs after the first introduction to the church family.—A missionary father.

Don't expect too much of them just because they are MKs.—A missionary mother.

Love Through a Warm Welcome
Southern Heights Church, Russellville, Kentucky, wrote to Don and Holly before we arrived home. When we did arrive the kids already knew people in their own classes at school, and of course Southern Heights was our choice for a church home.—Jenny (Mrs. James D.) Musen, Kenya.

In our church not one young person came to greet or meet our fourteen-year-old the night we joined. The church had approximately 1,000 members.—A missionary father.

My husband's home church has welcomed us "with two hands" [as they say in Malawi] and has made us feel welcome. They have loved us, shared with us, and not demanded too much of us. They have let us get the rest that we needed. They have helped the children to share things about Malawi without putting them in the spotlight.— Barbara (Mrs. Gerald M.) Workman, Malawi.

Love Through a Desire to Form Friendships and Be a Friend

Be friendly and interested in me!—An MK from Paraguay.

Since the teen years seem to be hardest to form new close friendships, it was such a blessing for the church teens to introduce themselves and include ours in activities immediately. They were shown their schools, Sunday School Departments, etc., etc.—LaQuita (Mrs. J. Wendell) Powers, Taiwan.

While on a summer furlough, not one young person offered friendship to our sons, although various mothers kept promising their sons were going to drop by. I don't blame the church entirely as our sons are content with each other's company and weren't outgoing at that age.—A missionary mother.

The friends at church were their best friends, and their social activities revolved mostly around church activities and those friends. Joining a girl's basketball team at church has been a real help in deepening friendship.—Ginger (Mrs. Don J.) McMinn, South Korea.

The first three weeks were miserable for our children as they knew no one; that opened the door to a great year for our children in their furlough home church. Also, our whole family of six were involved in the choirs which meant much to all of us. Our residence was located near the church and was almost always half filled with young people from the church.—A missionary father.

"Teachers were friendly," Julia said. "Church kids were friendlier than school kids."—Judy (Mrs. Darrel E.) Garner, Malawi.

Our church took two of our daughters with them on a trip to Ridgecrest. That same year the church we belonged to helped in many ways to make our children feel welcome. One of the best things we felt was going back to the same town for three furloughs. Friends in the church and town were friends again each furlough. One daughter has since married one of the boys she met there. The church has followed through with scholarships for each of the children in college. Being in that church, First Baptist Church of Bryan, Texas, has given our children a sense of having a home in the States."—Nelwyn (Mrs. John C.) Raborn, Hong Kong.

The kids in the church had different values and priorities than our children and they never did fit in with the "crowd." Possibly this was more our children's fault than the churches, but they never found fellowship. It made us sad, but we did not know how to resolve the problem either and could only pray for them.—An MK father.

Furlough was difficult for our children. They did not feel a part of the church. The adults involved made every effort, but the children and young people their age did not include them as they had felt included overseas, called them foreigners.—An MK father.

This furlough experience has been the best:

1. Good Bible study with peers.

2. Friends their age.

3. Church friends who attend their school. This cuts down on isolation and strangeness they feel. They automatically feel strange because they don't always know how to respond to every situation.

4. Adult friends who take a special interest in them.—An MK mother.

Love Through Prayer Support

Churches are a great help to MKs financially. It's not easy on us, but their prayer support is the most important. It means the world to us to know there is someone there who really cares.—An MK from Rhodesia.

Love Through Involving Them

Invite them to do things with the church—attend socials, etc. Try to get MKs actively involved in church programs (Acteens, etc.).—An MK from South Korea.

They could pay more attention to the MK and get him involved so that he can blossom out and grow spiritually, also maybe help out a little financially when needed.—An MK from South Brazil.

On our second furlough they were included in planning and carrying out youth activities. Individual families assumed responsibility for helping each child adjust to the North American life-style.—A missionary mother.

Love Through Inviting Them into Your Home

One lady in our church had all the Georgetown College MKs to dinner. It was neat!—An MK from Thailand.

I would appreciate visits from church staff, teachers, etc. and would like to be invited into their homes so I can feel more a part of the church.—An MK from Spain.

There are so many ways in which you can show your love. Perhaps the greatest is by simply giving them your attention. As one MK put it, "Sometimes it is best not to be treated as special, but then again I enjoy it sometimes."

It has been said that there are two great truths in each of us, "I need you, and I need to feel needed by you." This certainly applies here. The MK both needs your love and needs to feel that you want to love him. They are no different from anyone else.

Keeping in Touch

Furloughs do not last forever. They pass rather quickly, and soon the missionary family is leaving to return to the field. They may not return for four years. What will become of those friendships they have formed with their peers in the US?

From another perspective, what would it be like to write to an MK you do not know in the field and establish a relationship in this manner?

Some MKs felt little or no inclination to become involved in long-term correspondence and had no desire for it, yet others would eagerly become involved in letter writing and would welcome it.

They wrote letters and kept in touch a bit telling what the youth group was doing. It was great to stay in touch with those friends and even better when I got back to the US. They're like a second home.—An MK from Indonesia.

It would help keep us in touch with the people our age in the US.—An MK from Belgium.

I would have enjoyed it if someone could have written to me and shared what they did, what they studied, what the weather was like, what they wore, and what they did at church.—An MK from India.

Some wrote letters individually, and one group sent me a box of books.—An MK from Uruguay.

I had many friends from my youth group, pastor, and youth director who kept in touch with me overseas. That was great! I had some neat friendships through mail that were still very much alive when I got back to the US. I needed that contact with the States.—An MK from Kenya.

I asked missionary parents the question, "Do you have a church in the US which maintains a relationship with your child overseas? If yes, what form does it take? If no, do you feel it would be helpful, and what would you recommend?"

Here are some of their responses:

No, but it would be helpful by monthly letters.

Yes, our daughter did Acteen steps through cooperation with a church in Georgia.

Yes, packages of things unobtainable here were sent,

VBS jersys with the girls names printed on the back, and
their birthdays were printed in the church newsletter.—
Keith H. Williams, Philippines.

"No, they promised to do so, but they soon forgot. It
rather hurt our eldest son as he had looked forward to
keeping in touch. He learned, as we all learn, that very
few people in the US write personal letters."

"Yes, remembering birthdays and Christmas and food
packages which are *dear* to my children, a very positive
influence!"

Yes, Wauchula Baptist Church in Florida regularly
sends letters and packages on special days. Though we've
never met these people we feel their love and concern
and feel there are more churches just like them who are
caring for us also."—Phil and Oretha Brewster, Philippines.

Yes, our home church has often sent the kids cards,
small gifts or mainly just keeping in touch with someone
back home that is interested. It is excellent for them. It
gives the MK something to look forward to on furlough,
just another touch with the USA which they need to have
to be able to identify once they return.—Brenda (Mrs.
Paul D., Jr.) Lee, Spain.

No, not really. We do have a church which maintains a
relationship with the whole family. But as far as the kids
to kids, no. I do not recommend that you start some correspondence relationship which is based upon "Let's write
to the missionary kids" as some kind of different people.
They need and want normal relationships.—A missionary
father.

No, it would be helpful. Maybe they could send the
youth bulletin, other info, and snapshots. Maybe they
could even come see us.—James C. Oliver, Jr., Colombia.

Yes, a church in Missouri and Colorado honored them
with a special letter and graduation gift when they gradu-

ated from high school.—Janet (Mrs. Dale C.) Lindstrom, Venezuela.

One teenager offers this challenge—fitting, and worthy of remembering:

And when the furlough is over and they return with their parents to the mission station, we've got to pray for them specifically—for them and their schools, for their teachers as well as for their missionary parents. After all, these kids really are an important part of the program of world missions, even though they're no different from the kids we see on . . . [television] reruns.[45]

Notes

1. Donny Lockerbie, "Missionary Kids Are Just Kids," *Eternity*, Mar. 1976, p. 23. Reprinted by permission of *Eternity* Magazine, Copyright 1976, Evangelical Ministries, Inc., 1716 Spruce St., Philadelphia, PA 19103.

2. Mary Ann Ward, "Family Weekend Away from Home," *Royal Service*, Nov. 1974, p. 9.

3. Ibid., p. 9.

4. Marie McKay, "God Bless the Missionaries," *Royal Service*, Apr. 1983, p. 40-41.

5. Linda B. Kines, "The Shock of Coming Home," *The Commission*, Aug. 1971, p. 12.

6. Norman Jameson, " 'Missionary Kids' Feel God Calling 'Home,' " *Baptist Standard*, Apr. 13, 1983, p. 13.

7. Ibid.

8. Ibid.

9. Maureen D'Honau, "Question of the Week," *The Japan Times*, 29 Aug. 1976.

10. Truman Smith to E. V. May, Jr., Sept. 19, 1972.

11. Ruth Fowler, "Just a Title," *The Commission*, Apr. 1975, p. 18.

12. Ibid.

13. D. Bruce Lockerbie, *Education of Missionary's Children: The Neglected Dimension of World Missions* (South Pasadena, Cal. William Carey Library, 1976), p. 27.

14. Marjorie A. Collins, *Manual for Accepted Missionary Candidates* (South Pasadena, Cal.: William Carey Library, 1972), p. 11.

15. Mary Ann Ward, "MK Letters," *Accent*, July 1975, p. 27.

16. Johnnie Schoolar, "MKs Reflect Upon MC Life," *Mississippi Collegian*, Oct. 18, 1974.

17. Ibid.

18. Catherine Marshall, *Beyond Ourselves* (New York: McGraw-Hill Book Co., Inc.), 1959, p. 47-48.

19. Lorene Miley, "God Bless Our Missionaries . . . and Help the MKs Too," *Heartbeat*, Sept.-Oct. 1971, p. 3.

20. Maureen D'Honau, "Question of the Week," *The Japan Times*, Sept. 5, 1976.

21. Ward, "Family Weekend Away from Home," p. 9.

22. Stanley D. Stamps, "MK Roots," *The Commission*, Jan. 1975, p. 5.

23. Ibid.

24. Ibid.

25. Ward, "Family Weekend Away from Home," p. 9.

26. Ray F. Davis, "A Look at the Third Culture Child," *The Japan Christian Quarterly*, (Spring 1976), p. 67.

27. Laura S. Lane, "Missionary Kids Share Their Feelings About Being MKs," Mimeographed, Carson-Newman College, Jefferson City, Tenn. 1976, p. 6.

28. Lockerbie, "Missionary Kids Are Just Kids," p. 23. Used by permission.

29. Davis, "A Look at the Third Culture Child," p. 67.

30. D'Honau, "Question of the Week," 29 Aug. 1976.

31. Jameson, " 'Missionary Kids' Feel God Calling Home," p. 13.

32. Ibid.

33. Miley, "God Bless Our Missionaries . . . and Help the MKs Too," p. 3.

34. Gail Shiner, " 'Third Culture Kids' Feel Like Foreigners in Their Own Country," *Richmond Times Dispatch*, 8 Dec. 1974.

35. Ibid.

36. Truman Smith to E. V. May, Jr.

37. Shiner, "Third Culture Kids."

38. Ibid.

39. Miley, "God Bless Our Missionaries . . . and Help the MKs Too," p. 3.

40. O'Honau, "Question of the Week," 29 Aug. 1976.

41. Lockerbie, "Missionary Kids Are Just Kids," p. 23.

42. David Elkind, *The Hurried Child: Growing Up Too Fast Too Soon* (Reading, Mass.: Addison-Wesley Publishing Company, 1981), p. 3.

43. Nancy Blevins Ryals, "Missionary Families," *Royal Service*, Jan. 1977, p. 23.

44. Kines, "The Shock of Coming Home," p. 13.

45. Lockerbie, "Missionary Kids Are Just Kids," p. 23.

6

A Time for Adjustment: The MK and His College Experience

There comes a time in the life of missionaries when they must face the fact that their child is leaving home for college, and they may not see him for one year to several years. It has been called "The Greatest Sacrifice"[1] and has also been referred to as the "Separation Syndrome."[2] One missionary wrote, "Nothing in our experience in the field equals it."[3] It has also been referred to as one of the major factors leading to resignations by foreign missionaries.[4]

Time has a way of flying quickly by with the final day of departure arriving far too soon, yet all know it is going to happen. Most missionaries take steps of some kind to prepare their sons and daughters for that day.

Areas of Parental Preparation

When I asked the question of missionaries around the world, "Did you make any special effort to prepare your children for their adjustment to college, and, if so, what areas did you emphasize?" 81 percent said, "Yes, we made a special effort" while 14 percent said no with 5 percent uncertain. Most missionaries emphasized these areas:

Spiritual

We tried to prepare them spiritually for college by teaching them the importance of prayer, Bible study, a quiet time, and a daily walk with the Lord. We encouraged them to find a local church, join it soon, and become a part of its program. We encouraged them to join the BSU and find Christian young people to fellowship with. It was their choice though.—Sam and Ginny Cannata, Sudan.

Before college our emphasis was on a family altar daily, reading completely through the New Testament from *Good News for Modern Man* (The New Testament in Today's English Version), together. They had to memorize Scriptures and say them to us. Our oldest read through the New Testament, I think, eleven times. We encouraged very strongly their having a quiet time and the fact that Mom and Dad's relationship to God wasn't enough for them.—Doris (Mrs. Harry B.) Garvin, Uganda.

Financial

We let her open her own checking account at the bank and taught her to budget her allowance and balance her check book.—Ed Moses, Jr., Bophuthatswana.

I just talked with them about handling their finances, how to operate a bank account, and to get in touch with the FMB if they had any exceptional financial need or problem.—Loren C. Turnage, Scotland.

Emotional

"I informed my daughter that college life can have severe strains. I urged her to begin looking for possible helpers in the event that she should need them and urged her to be kind to herself in this regard rather than demanding."

"We learned through experiences of our first two children that helping a child to be independent in the US must begin long before they leave for college. As a result, our third child adjusted more easily."

"I tried to express confidence in his ability to fend for himself, and he began to look on it as an adventure."

"We tried to help them develop a relationship with their relatives so they would feel free to contact them and feel at home with them when they went to visit."

Academic

"We gave them ample opportunity to develop personal initiative in their study habits and use of study time."

"We taught them to spend time in study as well as activities. Learn to live with books as well as with people."

Some spoke with regrets:

"We emphasized money, sex, and church. We failed to deal with the drug problem."

"We should have done more. We probably didn't realize how completely unknown college life was to them. I think we could have helped them a great deal more."

Another represents many who came to understand the value of their preparation years later.

"Social, economical, and religious areas were emphasized, but we were not always successful at that time. Now, looking back over these experiences ten years later, we can see where we succeeded."

Others spoke about preparing their children at an early age:

It is early but I'm making that preparation now at ages nine, ten, and eleven. We follow the college life of Venezuelan MKs. Even now he [Roddy] has ideas of what to expect and is accepting going to that foreign country—USA—to study.—Katie (Mrs. Dean) Harlan, Venezuela.

We're working on it. As a junior in high school, we're making a special file of recipes that are easy and economical. He does some of his own laundry and handles his money on a monthly basis.—Lynn (Mrs. Jerry W.) Barrett, Hong Kong.

Still others spoke of how special retreats were planned for the purpose of preparing MKs for college. Basically, the areas covered are the same.

Patricia (Mrs. James M.) Wolf of Taiwan described the retreat from her role as "architect."

Preretreat testing includes PF-16 Personality Inventory and the Kuder Vocational Preference Examination. At the retreat, a trained counselor uses these tests to work with the group and then individually in interviews and follow-up if needed. Other areas covered at the retreat are (1) financial, (2) problem solving, (3) dating and roommates, and (4) what the FMB provides. One of our leaders set up a finance session in which each child was given $100.00 and then presented with a number of things to spend it on but only seeing one or two at a time by flipping chart pages: (1) room or dorm, (2) church, (3) refrigerator, (4) phone, (5) student activity, (6) parking and car pass, (7) books, etc. It was quite effective. It has proved to be a delightful weekend. Parents and students alike have been high in their praise.

As referred to in chapter 2, William G. Tanner makes seven excellent suggestions in preparing for the college experience. They are:

1. Prepare your child and yourself for the separation.

2. Decide in advance who will be the authority figure in the USA.

3. Not only establish a family figure, but try to find someone, if it is not the same person, close enough to your son or daughter so that he or she can have someone come to visit them on parent's day.

4. Help your young person to understand himself or herself.

5. Reorient your person to the USA.

6. Pray for your MK.

7. Accept the fact that he or she is going to change.[5]

Truman Smith speaks to the MK's departure in an article entitled "Open Letter to High School MKs" suggesting that they include at least these following five areas in the farewells: (1) say good-bye to the place that has been home, (2) say good-bye to your friends and peer group, (3) say good-bye to relationships that are as complete and up-to-date as possible, (4) include the mission and your local church in your good-byes, and (5) give special emphasis to your family good-byes.[6]

To be certain, preparation for college is most important, but also not to be neglected is what becomes of the MK after graduation.

One mother shared, "Maybe we talked too much about this and not enough about life after college. One of our sons asked us one day, 'What do you do after you finish four years in college and get your degree?' "

Six generalizations for MKs beginning their college experience have been drawn as a result of the research of Useem and others at Michigan State.[7]

1. They have trouble adjusting to the role of simply being an individual rather than a representative of an alien culture, a nation, or a religious group. These young people may have spent a lifetime being identified as Amerikajin, only to find that they feel themselves strangers to some extent in their homeland.

2. They exhibit a slightly higher than average dropout rate in the freshman year—though most return to complete their degree.

3. They may marry early (especially males), perhaps because they do not relate easily to groups. Early marriage would be a logical extension of the reliance on one close friend.

4. They are often shocked by what seems to them to be the prevalence of immoral and/or frivolous behavior among their classmates. This may lead to disillusionment with the entire college experience if not with society at large.

5. They find it difficult to pursue interests developed while overseas, such as language study.

6. They feel more cosmopolitan than their campus peers and have difficulty identifying people with whom they share interests. They often find their friends among the foreign students on their campus.

Those first days in the life of a college freshman are difficult enough whether or not the person is an MK. When you add in their relative isolation from the culture for the past several years, the lack of a parental base to fall back on, and limited finances it becomes especially difficult.

Let's hear MKs describe in their own words their first impressions of college life.

First Impressions of College Life

Jeanne Smith from Londrina, Brazil said, "My first impression was: I don't want to be here." She went on to explain that "there were seven different ways of talking and dressing."[8]

Keith Stamps of Ecuador recalls his first impression, "Too many people were speaking English."[9]

Karen Roper of Jordan shared:

I thought that because I had already been away to school [boarding school], had grown up overseas, and had traveled all over the world that I was a very independent young woman and could handle the world. But when I walked into my new dorm room with 44 pounds of luggage [two mere suitcases] and saw my roommate's color TV, expensive stereo, plush carpet, and a closet full of clothes, the American college life culture shock hit me right in the face.

Then I saw everyone else's parents helping them unpack, taking pictures, and hugging good-bye, I felt more alone than I had felt in my entire life. I realized going to college, especially as an MK, was not easy.

It is not an easy experience, and it affects MKs in different ways. Some have relatively few problems adjusting, while for others it will be more painful. What are some of the problems MKs face in college? Let's examine a few of the more common problems.

Common Problems for MKs in College

Separation

Keith Stamps refers to this difficulty: "My biggest problem is being away from my parents. It is difficult to be so far away from home and our families when friends go home and visit their parents every weekend or complain about not having seen their parents for two or three weeks. MKs really know what it means to go out on their own."[10]

Leslie Parkman, an MK from the Philippines, affirmed: "When no one else saw my dreams and my place in them, they always did. They encouraged my intellectual pursuits and applauded my academic attainments. I needed their continual spurring."[11]

As I read through hundreds of comments and responses to questions I had asked missionary parents and MKs alike, I was impressed with how many had mentioned that the furlough was planned in order that the family would be together through that first year of college. They could not speak highly enough of what this had meant to the parents and to the MK. Unfortunately, this may not always be possible. What are the alternatives?

One parent might accompany the MK for a few weeks to help with the adjustment. This is both temporary and very expensive as parents must pay for their own transportation.

The MK may have a satisfactory relationship with relatives to enable him to maintain a base away from home.

David Stewart, a missionary to Africa and now a Board-certified psychiatrist, wrote:

You who are missionary supporters are partly responsible for maintaining the contacts that keep ties right and foundations firm. Letters, pictures, and tapes will all help. Enhancing furlough contacts with time and money is well spent in brief visits, so that experiences are shared and boundaries are noted by small and developing people. Sometimes there really may be no extended family with whom to relate, yet the premise is still valid. Parents—even just one parent—can instill within the child the healing, nourishing certainty of who he is and see that he bears the clan name with pride and honor. Relatives and friends at the home base have special opportunities and obligations in situations like this.[12]

It may be that the MK will not be able to have that relationship with his relatives that he desires. Truman Smith commented, "Often family expectations may put more pressure on the college young person than is realized. That is, an aunt or an uncle may feel extremely responsible and not be as relaxed and understanding as a non-family member."[13]

Illness, distance, and age may also be negative factors influencing the MK's relationship with grandparents, aunts, and uncles.

This is where you the readers come in.

Why not offer to "adopt" an MK who is away at college, preferably a college close to you. Open your home to them and treat them like your own, not smothering or pitying them but loving them like your own. Give them a place to come home to on weekends and/or holidays. Remember their birthdays and special occasions. You could even assist them with finding a job. Write their parents and let them know of this new relationship. It will mean so much to them.

Eunice Short, who, with her family, has been involved in reaching out to MKs at Oklahoma Baptist University, shared these thoughts concerning the idea of adoption:

Families not living on a college campus could do a real service by writing to the college nearby, securing the names of the MKs, and writing and offering one or more of them an Oklahoma home for the period of time they are in college. They enjoy leaving town when the other students leave. They like to think that there is someone they can invite when there is an "Open House for Parents." Personally, I have toured dormitories many times, so the MKs here would feel that they had someone who cared on that day when the other students h ad family members coming. No one wants to feel left out. Certainly couples that do not have college age children would find this an enjoyable activity and one that would help to lengthen the vision of their young children and let them know someone from another part of the world.

She added that it helps MKs to have someone close to their parents' age. "I saw one family in Tulsa do such a splendid piece of work with three MKs from Africa. This young couple became the 'American Parents' and did so much for these young folks. I would like to see other couples follow in their footsteps."[14]

I might add, so would I!

There are still other ways that individuals help to fill the void left by parents. Many MKs have been helped financially.

One shared, "A Sunday School class adopted me as an MK. All during high school and college the class sent me $20.00 per month. They will never know how often that check bailed me out." Another said, "A Sunday School class gave me $25.00 so I could call 'home.' " Still another related, "A WMU in Rising Star, Texas, adopted me during my Baylor days and sent a care package every once in awhile. Cookies, a surprise gift, a card on my birthday were always warmly received, and they made me feel that someone cared, even though they didn't know me."[15]

As David Stewart put it so well, "Only you, as missionary family supporters, know if, as members of the extended mission family, you are being what you need to be for that mission family related to you by blood, or by God's direction, or both. Possibly you know a lonely MK somewhere whose parents are a world away. Perhaps there is one who needs advice, or a hug, or money, or a vacation with your family. Maybe you could send a missionary family a letter with pictures about hometown and family doings. In the process you may make the Christian family more consistent, may give the word *Christ* a special meaning to someone in need."[16]

Academics

Charles F. Kemp in his book *Counseling with College Students* cited a study conducted at Ohio State University and the University of Colorado which shows that academic problems are more prevalent than any other problem for the college student.[17]

Part of that problem may be due to how the MK handles his new sense of responsibility as one MK testified:

"The hardest thing was that I had to depend on myself. If I didn't feel like getting up for class, no one worried about it, and I think that is the first time I had that much responsibility placed on me. It was a hard adjustment in a way, but I think I've gotten used to it now."[18]

The inability of the student at the moment to adjust, discipline himself in study, and succeed academically can create a serious problem resulting in withdrawing from the college or university.

In his first semester of college an MK wrote his parents:

" 'These grades are not the best of my ability, I know,

but I find that I am not ready for college. I want to work awhile and get adjusted to the United States and Americans as they are *here*. I find myself unable to settle problems, adjust, and still make good grades at the same time.' "[19]

How do MKs compare academically with their peers? They compare quite favorably. As we saw earlier, the vast majority of MKs receive an excellent education overseas. Many parents and MKs felt it to be superior to that received in the US.

In comparison with other American students who have grown up overseas, the result is also quite favorable.

One doctoral dissertation which examined academic adjustment to college in the United States produced this typology:

(1) Federal civilian dependents (largely children of diplomats)

(2) MKs

(3) Business dependents

(4) Department of Defense civilians[20]

Though they ranked second in percentage of those receiving high grades, they had the lowest percentage claiming high self-concepts of intellectual ability. It was hypothesized that the work ethic held by these students led them to regard any grade below an *A* as evidence of less than adequate effort.[21]

Identity

David Stewart referred to identity as "that one factor of importance. That factor is individuation, the process of becoming, especially in our own view, an identifiable human with personal characteristics of importance and value."[22]

Robert F. Peck took all the different types of personality patterns in college students and placed them in three groups:[23] low, average, and high.

1. Characteristics of the low group:

(1) Many intense, primitively self-centered desires.

(2) Strongly conflicting feelings about major aspects of life.

(3) Relatively poor forethought to self-discipline.

(4) Destructive interpersonal behavior.

2. Characteristics of the average group:

(1) They are dependent social conformists.

(2) They get along half ineptly on a rather thin diet of human happiness and healthy pride.

(3) Most of them show a pervasive anxiety, of a tolerable but uncomfortable kind.

3. Characteristics of the higher group:

(1) They are strongly motivated to build self-realizing lives.

(2) They have diversified personalities, well developed on many sides.

(3) They experience powerful emotions gladly and find life deeper and easier for it.

(4) They think clearly and farsightedly.

(5) They are integrated people.

(6) They are genuinely ethical in their motives and in their behavior.

(7) They like other people, and others seek their company.

(8) These young people, too, have problems.

MKs are no different from their peers. All students encounter problems along the way. A study by Frances R. Robinson revealed that students will mark an average of twenty-five problems in areas such as adjustment to college life, personal psychological relations, vocational and educational failure, social and recreational activities, health and physical development, curriculum or teaching procedures, social-psychological relations, courtship, sex, marriage, finances, living conditions and employment, home and family, morals and religion.[24]

Through it all the MK's sense of self-worth will develop. As one MK so wisely said, "The main thing that is most important going through all of this is to be yourself, be who you are. If you are a banana-eater from Africa, be a banana-eater from Africa. Being able to accept yourself, self-acceptance is so important. We know what we think about ourselves and we know how we are, but we don't know how everyone else is. Learn to accept yourself. That's the most important thing." And that is what they do and do well.

Some MKs will go through an identity crisis, and it will likely be painful for all involved.

The dean of one Baptist college commented that as a whole MKs are well adjusted, "but occasionally we get one or two" that don't seem to adjust.[25]

One parent told of how his son withdrew completely during the freshman year, let his hair grow long, and went barefoot. But one day, realizing this was no way to behave, he made a complete turnaround, rededicated his life to the Lord, and today is active in Christian service.[26]

While leading a personal growth seminar for the Brazilian Home Mission Board, I met a young man who went through a most difficult identity crisis. He was born in Brazil, attended Brazilian schools, and received supplemental education through American correspondence courses. He spent his last two years of high school at Berry Academy in Rome, Georgia. His straight-A record brought him a scholarship to Emory University in Atlanta. He became involved with drugs. Eventually, a failed course doomed any further plans in medical school. His concerned parents sent him a ticket home, and he returned to Brazil where he taught English sporadically

" 'just enough for expenses and to keep myself in drugs.' "
His parents discovered the source of their son's problems
which resulted in numerous arguments. They considered
resigning or taking a leave of absence but eventually decided to stay.

After a year, Jimmy returned to the States and attended
Stetson University, DeLand, Florida, for two years. But
drugs remained a constant problem.

He dropped out of school and worked as a janitor. "I
was really pretty much disgusted with myself. I said,
'Here you are, Jim—you set out to be a doctor and now
you are a janitor.' That shows what drugs will do for you."

During a fraternity party he became desperate and
asked God to show him a plan for his life. He immediately
turned in the Bible to the Great Commission. Recalls
Moon, "It was a shock, and I said, 'No way.' I wanted
peace, I wanted forgiveness. I wanted the Lord to help
me straighten out my life, but I wanted to control. As a
result, I dove even deeper into drugs, trying to forget all
of this."

He sold a stamp collection and solicited gifts (Woman's
Missionary Union Executive Director Carolyn Weatherford, then with the Florida WMU, was among those who
helped), raising enough money to return to Brazil.

Being back in Brazil only brought more drug use and
more conflict with his parents. He finally got a job on an
oil rig.

Still miserable, he traveled to a resort island to think. A
cloud formation he saw seemed shaped like God's finger
pointing toward the sky. When he started to smoke
marijuana, he felt his mother was praying for him. He
asked God for a sign.

"When I finished praying, I saw where a tree had fallen.

One of the limbs was forming the One Way sign, so I went over to look; there were a lot of holes in that branch, and where the palm of the hand would have been was this very big hole, as if it were where the nail pierced the Lord's hand.

"At that moment I felt the Lord really was with me. I knelt down and prayed, and I felt the presence of the Lord. I gave him my life, and he started to work."

He threw the marijuana away.

"After that I still went back to drugs once or twice, I still smoked cigarettes some and still drank a couple of times, but the Lord was working—and he freed me."

Out of all this he clarified a call to become a missionary. He preached his first sermon in a Rio de Janeiro church. Two persons accepted Christ that night. He was graduated from South Brazil Baptist Theological Seminary and became a home missionary.[27]

The young man's name is Jimmy Moon, the son of missionaries Loyd and Mary Hazel Moon, and one of the finest and most dedicated young men I know.

When one MK is hurting, we all hurt though the pain is felt most keenly by those more closely involved. God is at work throughout the circumstances, and He will likely in His way use others to reach out to that MK.

I like what William Tanner wrote in the conclusion of "Strictly Personal for Parents of MKs." Though pertaining to the university setting, I believe it is just as applicable for those who love and know MKs. He wrote,

"I want to assure the missionaries, and especially the missionary parents that most of the people I know who serve in Baptist colleges and universities are ready to walk the second, third and fourth mile to make the adjustment back to the States as successful as it can possibly be for our MKs."[28]

For those who have not related so closely to MKs, my prayer would be that you will make that effort.

Dating

Though dating was discussed in depth in "The Coming Home Shock," it bears repeating briefly here for it can be a problem for the MK.

Franklin Fowler related how some MKs have told him they are "literally scared to death" of dating in the United States. Questions like 'How do you act?', What time should you come in?', and 'How do you dress?' are more than mere inquiries about etiquette. Many girls have a strict, fundamental upbringing. They are familiar with church parties and holding hands, but that is about as far as it goes."[29]

Dancing is another problem for many MKs. They are often faced with handling this social situation, common in the States, without going against their upbringing.[30]

Some parents will prepare their children for the challenges prior to their departure to begin college. Some MKs will find help from other MKs, yet others will seek out one or more persons who will be able to provide necessary information.

Church

The church does enter the picture as a problem for some MKs. Let's look at it from three different perspectives: (1) the worship service, (2) expectations of the MK, and (3) demands upon the average member.

Several MKs found it difficult to be a part of a larger church. Having come from smaller churches with less members than those in the US, they felt the churches here were too large and/or impersonal.

Concerning the worship service one mentioned that his church service was televised every Sunday, and it was hard for him to have a worship experience with the cameras and speakers everywhere. The emphasis on numbers and size was also a problem for him.

In regard to expectations another MK felt pressure in being an example, feeling like she "had to perform and do everything when at church." Mary Ann Ward wrote that some "feel pressure to be active in a church because it is expected of them."[31]

Perhaps it is the contrast in life-styles, as much as anything else, that creates a problem for the MK. Linda Kines wrote:

MKs are often shocked at what they find in stateside Baptist churches.

An MK may be familiar with people losing their reputation and even their lives to become Christians in another country. Then he attends an air-conditioned church in the States and sees deacons who can hardly wait to step outside for a cigarette when the service is over.[32]

However, just as the church may pose a problem to the college age MK as he returns to the States, it can also be that healing balm that he needs as he makes his own place in a land he has never really been able to know well.

I asked MKs this question: "At this point in terms of your identity as a college student, do you feel that the local church where your college is located is meeting your spiritual needs? If not, is it a problem of the church, self, or both? What do you think is the answer to the problem, and what can be done?"

Sixty-seven percent responded that the local church was meeting their needs spiritually, while 33 percent said it was not. Let's begin with the latter percentage as we try to understand the problem a little more clearly.

Most MKs who responded negatively felt it was more a problem of self than the church.

1. The pressure to fulfill that "image"—"maybe it is my own fault. I'm tired of everyone being overconcerned about my life. Maybe they just expect too much in stereotypes."

2. Situational circumstances—"I do not really want to go to this church, but my parents spoke there when I first entered college, and the pastor's family as well as the congregation have been very nice to me, so I feel obligated to go there. I suppose the reason I don't like to go there is because I feel pressured to attend."

3. Comparison to their church in another part of the world—"I relate back to my church in Brazil too much and compare the two. I should not do this, but I do, and it causes me to *not* appreciate church here as much."

4. Self-enforced isolation—"It might be my fault since I stay home to study on Wednesday and Sunday nights when I could really be helped."

Of course, it should not be overlooked that each of us must bear the responsibility for our own spiritual growth through daily prayer, Bible study, witnessing, and other factors. Some MKs were quick to point this out and rightly so.

Some MKs mentioned other negative reasons, such as the lack of depth in preaching, lack of missions mindedness in the church as a whole, and several others already set forth previously.

Some suggested that the problem was shared by the church and the MK.

"It's a problem of both. The churches I've visited have been very materialistic. I've been looking for a church that can compare to my church back home and have gone wrong in trying to find one just like it. I need to rely more on God for guidance instead of what kind of church I want. I need to look for where He wants me to be and what He wants me to do."

The majority felt the local church was meeting their spiritual needs from these perspectives.

1. Previous association with the church.—"The church that I am attending now is the church I attended for three years before this summer, and it has really been an asset in my Christian life."

2. The opportunity to be on the receiving end for a change.—"The church is really super, a good pastor, good music, and a good college department. It is so good that I don't have a place to serve. I'm used to having my part to do, and now I don't."

This feeling must be balanced with the attitude on the part of some who are frustrated because they *don't* have a place of service as the MK who said, "I'd like to get more involved—do something—I'd like to feel *used.*"

3. Familiarity with the language.—"I'm very happy at my church. I feel a special spiritual uplifting because I couldn't always understand all the Chinese sermons."

4. Well-organized college department and Sunday School class.—"My church has a wonderful college department. Our Sunday School class is very helpful, and I feel I'm growing spiritually through it."

5. The feeling of oneness with other students.—"The church where I attend seems to be doing all it can to make *all* college students welcome. They not only want us to come and worship, they want *us* to serve the church."

One MK said, "I asked the Lord to lead me to a really deep church, and He answered my prayer. I'm really happy with it."

As you have noticed by now, no names were used with the quotes. One or more quotes might be applicable to your church, hopefully from the positive side, but perhaps not. Our churches will only be as responsive as we ourselves permit them to be. The MK is no different in that he, too, needs ministering unto. We all do, and it is up to you and me to be doing this very thing.

The Ministry of the WMU

Like my colleagues, I am deeply indebted to the Woman's Missionary Union for all that has been done on behalf of missions around the world. This includes the missionary family and especially the MK.

I wrote to every WMU state director and president and asked them to give me information about what existing programs with MKs were in effect and how some churches in the state were involved in various programs with MKs. Responses from twenty-one states came in. Their answers were varied and interesting, from the highly organized state WMU which has an extensive program to the newly formed state WMU which would like to do more.

State WMUs have a list of MKs who are attending colleges and universities not only in their own state but throughout the US as well. This list is available from the Foreign Mission Board in Richmond, Virginia. The list identifies universities and colleges in each state where we have MKs, the addresses to correspond with them, their names, the countries they represent, and their birthdays.

I can include only a few examples of the vast work being done with and for MKs. The Florida WMU, for example, publishes a booklet entitled "Missionary Kid Birthday Calendar." In addition to listing the names of Florida home and foreign missionary children and their birthdays, it also lists suggested ways to help and become involved in their lives.

Bernice Elliott shared with me that the Birmingham, Alabama, association, under the leadership of the associational support director had led the churches of that association to do many things.

One is to provide wrappings, ribbons, boxes, and postage for a "Christmas wrapping party." Churches are enlisted to carry out this ministry. The young people bring their gifts, wrap them, get them ready for shipping, and munch on refreshments. The support chairman sees that the packages are shipped, and the postage is furnished from the associational WMU budget.[33]

The state WMUs of Texas and Oklahoma, among others, encourage associations and local churches in their ministry to MKs.

Both a fall and a spring retreat for MKs is held at the Oklahoma state GA and Acteen camp. This is but one of many different activities planned for MKs.

Ann (Mrs. Gerald) Pitman of Waco shared many projects that involve MKs in her area. Let me share two with you on the local church level in Waco.[34]

1. "First Baptist invited MKs to speak at their missions banquet during the week of prayer for foreign missions several years ago. As each MK came forward and was introduced, an RA brought a flag forward from the MK's country and placed it at the front of the room. The tables were decorated with items from countries around the world.

2. "For about eight to nine years, Columbus Avenue honored MKs, retired and furloughing missionaries in the morning worship service on the first Sunday of the week of prayer for foreign missions. The WMU hosted a luncheon for them in the fellowship hall afterwards. The MKs were given an airform so they could write home. Also, a group picture was made and each MK and missionary was given one."

Nearly all the WMUs assist MKs financially. It may be a check to each MK as the South Carolina WMU does three times a year (fall, Christmas, and Easter), the birthday of the MK as does the Arkansas WMU, or at Christmas as does the Mississippi WMU.

The Louisiana WMU offers a free scholarship as a gift. The children of Louisiana missionaries attending Louisiana College have the privilege of applying for one of these scholarships. The same holds true for young women who attend a Southern Baptist seminary.

Lottie R. Crion, President of the WMU in the Northern Plains Baptist Convention told me of a fund that I found most interesting. She described:

Our convention initiated a "LIFT fund" several years ago. The name is an acronym of "Love in Financial Terms." Throughout the year offerings from local WMU organizations, associational groups and at convention meetings are collected to produce the fund. At Christmas each year the amount available is divided equally between the children of foreign missionaries who claim one of our four states as "home" and the college/seminary attending children of each of our appointed home missionaries serving in the Northern Plains. The amount has varied from year to year, as has the number of recipients. All three of our children received a LIFT check each year while they were in college. They appreciated it very much, and that has been the response of all the MKs each year.[35]

Some states budget the amount to be sent, as does the Georgia WMU through the "Burney Gifts." Others take a special offering as does the Utah-Idaho Convention at their annual WMU/Brotherhood meeting in November.

The Missouri WMU established the Madge Truex Fund in 1953. The fund was previously known as the WMU Specials Fund. Named in honor of Mrs. C. M. Truex, executive secretary of Missouri WMU from 1936-1947, the fund is made up of donations given through the local church. The fund includes "Margaret Fund" students, children of home and foreign missionaries who are attending college in Missouri.[36]

The amount provided for each MK varies from state to state and from year to year. It may vary anywhere from $5.00 to $150.00.

As Miss Alberta Gilpin, state WMU director of Missouri, put it, "The letters we receive after sending those gifts are especially meaningful." She continued: "We know it does have a special meaning in some of their lives."[37]

The involvement through the local church can be quite supportive. The First Baptist Church of Bowling Green, Kentucky, reaches out to MKs through several groups of "Baptist Women" in the church.

Doris (Mrs. Ray) Mullendore related they have done these and many other things for MKs at Western Kentucky University:[38]

1. Helped to stock the pantry for an MK in his own apartment.

2. Supplied baked items and other "goodies" during special holiday times of the year.

3. Taken a baked item each week to the MK.

4. Invited the MK to the home for a meal and family involvement.

Mrs. Joanne Dowler, from First Baptist Church of Los Alamos, New Mexico, related, "In the fall of 1982 the daughter of a missionary couple to Japan was married in our church to the son of a church member. Because the bride and groom were unknown in our church and because the MK's parents could not come for the wedding the Baptist women helped with the reception and also gave the couple gifts."[39]

Willie Merle (Mrs. H. P.) Lawrence, office secretary at the WMU headquarters in Brentwood, Tennessee, shared with me an extremely inovative program of "MK adoption":

"In 1982 Miss Jannie Engelmann, our GA director, drew up a plan for GA organizations in the churches to 'adopt an MK,' and presented it to those who attended the 'G-A-las' in October and November." She enclosed a page with four requirements for adoption of a missionary kid, the "adoption contract," the "adoption certificate," and a list of twenty-two GA organizations which have adopted an MK.[40] [See Appendix.]

One other program of interest is that entitled "Cousins." In the words of Dick Rader, its sponsor at Oklahoma Baptist University:

"Cousins" is a fairly loose-knit organization which seeks to meet the needs of the MKs. However, we try to avoid being a clique or closed group. We are registered with our campus government. Some years we don't meet as often as we do at other times. We try to do all the MKs want to do without trying to be too much for them.

In addition to the two retreats (fall and spring, fully provided by the state WMU and the Brotherhood Department), we also have various other social functions: birthday parties, end-of-year pizza parties, and parties honoring our graduating seniors and engaged persons. We try to include furloughing, retired, or former missionaries who live nearby in some of our activities. Our OBU missionaries-in-residence are included in our meetings and retreats and at times we have invited other missionaries to join us.[41]

Concerning his part Dick said, "When MKs have problems, I try to be available."[42]

The Baptist Brotherhood

The Baptist Brotherhood also reaches out to MKs in various ways.

They have assisted in finding summer jobs for MKs—a popular request.

They also promote establishing relationships between

RAs and MKs through the "Royal Ambassador Advancement Plan" and program activities in weekly meetings held in churches across the United States and around the world.

The Baptist Brotherhood works closely with the Woman's Missionary Union in many states in programs of outreach to MKs.

The Foreign Mission Board

Truman Smith devotes full time to meeting with, listening and responding to members of missionary families. The Board has had a missionary family consultant office since 1971.

Ways missionary families are undergirded by Smith's office include:

MK Weekend: Thanksgiving, the first big holiday in the school year, can be a traumatic time for MK college freshmen in the United States. The Foreign Mission Board brings the MKs to Richmond for a weekend of fellowship, fun, and sharing.

The weekend has a "double focus," according to Smith. "It gives the MKs a time to be with people of kindred mind and spirit, and provides resources in the program structure to deal with concerns such as spiritual direction, vocation."

Margaret Fund: each child of a missionary family in current service is eligible to receive $1,700.00 annually for four years paid to their school and a supplement of $85.00 a month paid directly to the student eight times during the year. Prorated tuition amounts are provided for children of resigned missionaries with service of after ten years.

MKs in graduate school receive a one-year stipend of $1,000.00; it can be extended for two or three years if the student is in an M.R.E. or M.Div. program in a seminary.

Visit Home: Once during their college years, MKs are provided a trip to visit parents on the field.

Family Conferences: Various missions and their area offices work with Smith's office to hold Family Enrichment Conferences in central locations on their fields. Professionals in family topics are taken to these meetings so missionaries deal with concerns in their daily settings, Smith pointed out.

Other Resources: Smith's office works along with other Foreign Mission Board offices in providing information and assistance to missionary families. Furlough possibilities for personal and professional development are compiled by the FMB consultant for furlough study and conferences. Both Smith and the Board's medical consultant provide resources for physical, psychological, and psychiatric needs.

The intent is to complement and add to the Board's other support systems. The organization sees its relationship to missionaries as that of "enabler," Smith said, to the end that those on the field serve at a high level of effectiveness.[43]

Notes

1. Roy F. Lewis, "The Greatest Sacrifice," *The Commission,* Jan. 1975, p. 12.
2. M. E. Hill, "The Separation Syndrome," *The Commission,* Jan. 1975, p. 30.
3. Ted Cox, "Missionary Milestones: Family Separation," *Royal Service,* Aug. 1976, p. 11.
4. Lewis, "The Greatest Sacrifice," p. 12.
5. William G. Tanner, "Strictly Personal for Parents of MKs," n.d.
6. Truman S. Smith, "Open Letter to High School MKs," *Foreign Missionary Intercom,* Apr. 1981, p. 1.
7. Ray F. Downs, "A Look at the Third Culture Child," *The Japan Christian Quarterly* (Spring 1976), p. 67-68.
8. Johnnie Schoolar, "MKs Reflect upon MC Life," *Mississippi Collegian,* Oct. 18, 1974.
9. Ibid.
10. Ibid.

11. Leslie Parkman, "Switching from Rice to French Fries," *Contempo*, Jan. 1977, p. 4.

12. David Stewart, "To the Larger Family," *The Commission*, Jan. 1975, p. 9.

13. Truman Smith to E. V. May, Jr., Sept. 19, 1972.

14. Eunice Short to William C. Viser, Mar. 25, 1983.

15. Ann and Gene Pitman, "Ministering to Missionaries and Their Families," Mimeographed, Texas WMU Annual Meeting, Corpus Christi, 1982, p. 8.

16. Stewart, "To the Larger Family," p. 9.

17. Charles F. Kemp, *Counseling with College Students* (Englewood Cliffs: Prentice-Hall, 1964), p. 38.

18. Ruth Fowler, "The MK Perspective: Growing Up Overseas," *Contempo*, July 1976, p. 10.

19. Linda B. Kines, "The Shock of Coming Home," *The Commission*, Aug. 1971, p. 13.

20. Downs, "A Look at the Third Culture Child," p. 68.

21. Ibid.

22. Stewart, "To the Larger Family," p. 9.

23. Robert F. Peck, "Student Mental Health: The Range of Personality Patterns in a College Population," *Personality Factors on the College Campus*, eds. Robert T. Sutherland, Wayne H. Holtzman, Earl A. Koile, and Bert Kruger Smith (Austin, Texas: The Hogg Foundation for Mental Health, 1962).

24. Kemp, *Counseling with College Students*, p. 39.

25. Stanley D. Stamps, "MK Roots," *The Commission*, Jan. 1975, p. 6.

26. Ibid.

27. Mike Creswell, "He's Back in the Light," *The Commission*, Sept. 1981, pp. 12-17.

28. Tanner, "Strictly Personal for Parents of MKs."

29. Kines, "The Shock of Coming Home," p. 12.

30. Ibid.

31. Mary Ann Ward, "Family Weekend Away from Home," *Royal Service*, Nov. 1974, p. 9.

32. Kines, "The Shock of Coming Home," p. 13.

33. Bernice Elliott to William C. Viser, Mar. 28, 1983.

34. Mrs. Gerald G. Pitman to William C. Viser, Apr. 26, 1983.

35. Lottie R. Crim to William C. Viser, Mar. 9, 1983.

36. Woman's Missionary Union of the Missouri Baptist Convention, "Madge Truex Fund," Mimeographed, Missouri Baptist Convention, 1982.

37. Miss Alberta Gilpin to William C. Viser, Feb. 25, 1983.

38. Mrs. Doris Mullendore to William C. Viser, Mar. 10, 1983.

39. Mrs. Joanne Dowler to William C. Viser, Mar. 28, 1983.

40. Mrs. H. P. Lawrence to William C. Viser, Mar. 1, 1983.

41. Dick Rader to William C. Viser, Apr. 4, 1983.

42. Ibid.

43. Martha Skelton, "Missionary Families: Some Stresses and Strengths," *The Commission*, Dec. 1981, p. 16.

7
From the Heart:
MKs Speak Out
and Share Their Feelings

Relationships are what life is all about. Your relationship with Jesus Christ is central to who you are and what
you do.

Your relationship with your parents and brothers and/
or sisters had a profound influence on your life.

Who among us can ever know the influence of teachers
in the church and school, of pastors and staff members, of
friends?

I have only to reflect upon my own life to see how God
has ministered to me, shaped my life, and lovingly molded
me through people with whom I have had relationships;
and I believe God has used me in the same way.

I have enjoyed my contacts with MKs. MKs have been
a part of my life for longer than I can remember. I knew
them as a boy, I studied with them in college and seminary, I became an "MK uncle" upon our appointment as
foreign missionaries in 1978, and last, but certainly not
least, I am an MK father to my daughter, Lauren, and son,
Ryan.

I have had opportunities to listen to MKs the world over
from all denominations. I want to share with you here
their thoughts on some very important subjects: Christianity, missionary efforts, their relationship to Jesus
Christ, their view of the world today, their feelings toward those who support them in the United States, grow-

ing up overseas and what they would say to the parents of future MKs as well as to future MKs.

Christianity and Missionary Efforts

Should be spread in a personal, loving way.—Larry Welch, South Brazil.

Jesus is Lord, and the world needs to know. We are responsible for sharing.—Edward Ellison, Indonesia.

Another wrote, "Christianity is my life, and missions will always have a special place in my heart."

Christianity would be nothing without missions. Christ gave us 'the Great Commission.' If we do not here it, we are missing something that is very important in our Christian life.—Vera Hern, Jordan.

Relationship to Jesus Christ

I love Jesus so much, and I realize just how much I need Him when I'm on my own.—Kris Spenser, Philippines.

Growing closer everyday, but I want it to grow even stronger.—Janean Shaw.

It is the most important relationship I will ever have in my entire life.—Alan Robson, Liberia.

"The only thing that keeps me going in hard times."

"He is my Savior. I have yet to learn to make Him true Lord of my life."

Growing every day, and I love Him so much. He's my *whole* strength, especially since I no longer have my folks near by.—Martha Stewart, Kenya.

Hasn't been an easy road, but Jesus is growing me and teaching me many new things.—Debbie Greene, Taiwan.

The World Today

The world is crying out for love and help, and we as Christians must be the ones to answer that cry.—Cynthia Oliphint, Tanzania.

"A sad, sad mess, largely due to individual apathy. It makes me feel like crying."

Messed up and needs a lot of help. The missionaries can't do it all.—Vince Everhart, Korea.

"A mess with only one way to be straightened out—through Jesus Christ."

Those Who Support You

Super! I'm very grateful for their prayer and support. Thanks a bunch.—Bill Reynolds, Belgium.

"They are why I am what I am. I get upset with them sometimes, but I appreciate them."

Another expressed his feelings toward those who support him and his family without using words, though what he put down spoke volumes. He simply put out by the side of the question: #1.

Growing up Overseas

"I have a better outlook on the world. It's helped me form many opinions of what I think life is all about."

"It has matured me faster and more than my peers."

"Very much. I'm more knowledgeable of other places, and I find it easier to understand and talk to people."

"Growing up overseas has been one of the most important things that has happened to me in my life as a growing Christian."

To the Parents of Future MKs

"To spend more time with their kids and teach them early to be independent and to trust in the Lord."

"To raise MKs in a Christian home but not secluded from the world they have to live in."

"Give them a little room to do some thinking of their own."

"Don't be discouraged if your MKs learn the language before you do!"

"Pray for your MK and include your kids in quiet times."

"Although they may rebel [because many of us do] they'll come around, I did."

"Listen to your kids. There will be problems they will face overseas that they wouldn't have to face in the US. Be patient, and always ask God for guidance in helping your kids grow up."

"Try to understand. You will not fully do so because you will not have grown up as they have. Encourage them."

"Give your kids priority. The family was instituted before the church. Make sure your kids have a strong identity. Let them see advantages and disadvantages of other life-styles. Make sure they know you are really called by God."

The words of an Indonesian missionary Mom: "I don't know what the world will be like when my two grow up. The best security and love gift I could give them is to raise them up in the Lord, encouraging them in their relationship with Him."

"Have your kids get involved in the culture in which they are living, learn the language, and get to know the people. In other words, don't create a 'Little America,' in another country. *However*, do teach them their American heritage and background."

To Future MKs

It's a great opportunity. Take advantage of every moment.—Anita Brake, Paraguay.

While you'll miss your relatives, a whole, wide, exciting world is ahead of you—it's a great experience.—Amanda Blakely, Tanzania.

"Enjoy, but think of who you represent, your parents and Christ, before you do anything."

Your parents are there to help you grow. Don't take them for granted. They are worth really getting to know as good friends as well as being parents.—Thomas Kirkendall, Belgium.

"It's a pity that most of us can't appreciate our situation until we have left the mission field and look back in retrospect. Appreciate it *NOW!* You are special!"

"People have gone through what you are going through, so don't give up the ship. Many have had it harder, and no one said the going would be easy. Whenever you have a major problem, try to let the Board help you."

"Enjoy your foreign country when you are there. Enjoy the US when you're *there.*"

"Do not be afraid of your identity. Don't run away from it but develop it, and in a subtle way come through to people without 'proving' yourself. Be yourself always."

"Don't depend only on your parents' beliefs, know God for yourself."

"Get into the country you are in and make the most of it! Enjoy it! Don't reject the States totally either. Get the best of them all."

"It's a tough world, but if you are in a good relationship with the Lord you are heading for a super future."

"You have a definite advantage over most other kids. Use that advantage and your talents to their fullest potential."

"Always keep an open mind. Consider everything before rejecting it. Question how Christ would feel about it. Always keep Christ first in your life."

"It's great, and you are the most privileged kids. It may be hard at times, but it is worth it."

This is what I pray for the reader: that you might come to know a group of young people that are no different from your own. They have the same basic needs: love, security, and so forth. Don't try to stereotype them, because you cannot. Each one is a unique individual, and they are all worth knowing. Their life and certainly your life will be richer for it!

And I know that once you get to know them as I do, you too will be able to say, "It's OK to be an MK."

Appendix

What State WMU Leadership Can Do for MKs
(Margaret Fund Students)

1. Receive names of MKs who are Margaret Fund students from Home and Foreign Mission Boards:
   a. School attending
   b. From which country or US address
   c. MKs birthdays.
2. Send appropriate information to associational WMU presidents.
3. Encourage associational and local leadership to seek key churches and key persons for responsibilities regarding MKs.
4. Use state Baptist paper as well as bulletins to inform people in your state of names, addresses, and birthdays of MKs.
5. Upon request provide addresses of MKs.
6. Promote intercessory prayer for MKs on their birthdays. (Pray for MKs at other times, too.)
7. Explore the possibility of inviting MKs during Thanksgiving holidays to retreats with internationals (with exception of first-year MKs who go to Richmond for a retreat at Thanksgiving).
   If there is no international retreat in your state at Thanksgiving, plan for an MK get-together at Thanksgiving time.
8. Use MKs in state WMU annual meetings and conferences (for speaking, singing, instrumental music, etc.).
   Encourage other state convention departments to use them in a similar manner.
9. Include a budget item for MK ministry.
10. Encourage appropriate associations and churches to budget for MK ministry.
11. Send cards or letters to MKs on birthdays, at Christmas, and other occasions.
12. Think in terms of sending a gift of money at least once a year to the MKs in your state. (Perhaps the birthday would be a nice time to send it.)
13. At conferences provide an opportunity for those who are

working with MKs to talk and share regarding their MK ministry.

14. Sometime during the year (early as possible) write to the parents of MKs telling them of your friendship with their children, etc.

15. Share with your national WMU leadership any suggestions or ideas you have for MK ministry.

16. Write to new MKs—letting them know you anticipate their arrival for college. (Early in the summer contact your school offices for this information.)

17. Seek opportunities to get acquainted with MKs; be a loving listener.

What Associational WMU Leadership Can Do for MKs
(*Margaret Fund Students*)

1. Select (or elect) an individual, a couple (or committee), to the responsibility of directing MK ministry in the association.
2. Lead churches to "Adopt-an-MK" program, thus linking MKs to a family and home. Invite them often into your homes for meals, or for weekends.
3. Include MK ministry in budget.
4. Encourage appropriate churches to budget for MKs.
5. Use MKs at associational meetings or gatherings.
6. Arrange opportunities for MKs to get with internationals from their adopted countries.
7. Encourage development of MK talents—musical groups (instrumental and vocal). Make cassette tapes to send to parents.
8. Enable MKs to contact their parents by phone at Christmas time or on parents' birthdays. Enlist the HAM operators' interest in this project.
9. Open homes for MKs during campus holidays. (Check with school offices for information and dates.)
10. Plan well in advance for trips to interesting points, such as "Six Flags Over Georgia," museums, fairs; or for outing trips, skating, bowling, etc. Purchase tickets, provide food and transportation for these trips.
11. Lend assistance to MKs who need summer or vacation jobs.
12. Help MKs get settled at the beginning of the school year.
13. Take MKs shopping.
14. At Christmastime mail MKs' packages to their parents overseas. (In early October plan a Christmas "wrap-up" party. MKs bring the gifts—you provide wrapping paper, etc., party food.)
15. MKs could be helpful in churches by providing displays, leaflets, up-to-date information on missions around the world.
16. Use MKs at "World Missions Fairs."

17. Promote intercessory prayer for MKs on their birthdays. (Pray for MKs at other times, too.)
18. Plan with a local WMU for birthday cakes to be provided and delivered on MK's birthday.
19. Study well all suggestions on "local WMU sheet"—promote the ideas—think of additional ones then share with your state or national leadership.
20. Know MKs personally. Be a good and loving listener.

What Local Church WMU Leadership Can Do For MKs
(*Margaret Fund Students*)

1. Determine by election or selection who will be the individual, the couple, or the committee responsible for MK ministry.
2. Promote the "adopt-an-MK" program, thus linking MKs to a family and home. Have them often in your home for meals or for weekends.
3. Invite MKs (as well as internationals) into homes during school holidays.
4. Include a budget item for MK ministry.
5. Be aware of mission study topics for months ahead . . . invite as special guests MKs and internationals from these areas.
6. Provide occasions when all MKs can get together for a meal, a picnic, or just a social time in a home or at the church.
7. Cooperate in the planning of trips to interesting places, such as "Six Flags Over Georgia," state fairs, museums, operas, or for recreational trips—skating, bowling, swimming, etc. Purchase tickets, provide food and transportation for these trips.
8. Help students locate summer or holiday jobs, even jobs on Saturdays.
9. Remember MKs on special occasions—birthdays, graduations, Christmas, marriage, etc. (Perhaps a $10 bill; a gift certificate from Book Store; cassette tape of favorite music; magazine subscription of choice.)
10. Sometime during the school year (early as possible) write to the parents of MKs, telling them of your friendship with their children, etc.
11. Enable MKs to call home at Christmastime or on parents' birthdays. Enlist HAM radio operators' interest in this project.
12. Plan shopping trips for MKs. (Kids from tropics need warm clothes, will take one or two days in a shopping mall. Kids will have money—but would appreciate lunch.)
13. Arrange an "on-call" contact for MKs who need emergency assistance with medical, financial, legal questions.

14. Promote intercessory prayer for MKs on their birthdays. (Pray for MKs at other times, too.)

15. Arrange an "on-call" contact for MKs who need transportation to appointments, such as dentist, doctor, etc., or transportation from dorm to bus station, airport, etc.

16. Use MKs to keep an up-to-date display in churches of materials from mission fields, etc.

17. Use MKs during the weeks of prayer (Wednesday evening speaker, Sunday night, etc.).

18. Provide and deliver cakes on MKs' birthdays.

19. Frequently send "thinking of you" notes; something "homemade to eat;" note stationery; stamps or aerograms, a roll of quarters for the washing machine; small personal gifts, such as socks, panty hose, mending kit, soap, toothpaste, etc.

20. Provide a place to store the dorm room contents during vacations or during the trip back to the field.

21. By the middle of October have a "Christmas wrap-up party." MKs bring their gifts—you provide wrapping paper, ribbon—and postage to mail them to the field.

22. At all times be a good and loving listener.

Requirements For Adopting a Missionary Kid

1. It shall be the responsibility of the Girls in Action group, hereinafter known as GAs, to establish contact with their Missionary Kid, hereinafter known as MK, early in the year so that they can have a meaningful relationship with the adopted MK throughout the year.

2. An MK shall be adopted by the consent and commitment of a majority of the girls in a GA group.

3. The GAs who adopt an MK shall perform such deeds of love as any family performs for a son or daughter whom they love. This will include:

(a) remembering special events such as birthday, Christmas, graduation and other events in the life of the MK.

(b) praying regularly for the MK.

(c) visiting the MK at least once during the year and sending a letter to the parents of the MK to share with them about the visit. This visit could be done by inviting the MK to the church (and paying his/her expenses) for a special event or the GAs could make an appointment to visit the MK at his/her school (perhaps to take him/her out for a meal).

(d) sending a goodie box (home made cookies, candy, etc.) at least once during the year.

4. An adoption shall last for the period of 1 (one) year and may be extended to more years upon the mutual consent of both the MK and all the GAs.

[For more ministry ideas look on pages 12 and 13 of *Family Missions* by Oneta Gentry.]

Adoption Contract

WHEREAS, we believe that the Bible instructs us to "go into all the world and preach the gospel to every creature"; AND

WHEREAS, we are not able at this time to go to another part of the world; AND

WHEREAS, other Christians known as "Missionaries" have gone into other parts of the world but some have had to leave their sons and daughters here in the United States for the purpose of educating them; AND

WHEREAS all children need love and nurture;

THEREFORE, we, the undersigned, with love and concern for missions and for Missionary Kids do enter into this contract for the adoption of the Missionary Kid named below. We promise to fulfill the REQUIREMENTS FOR ADOPTION OF A MISSIONARY KID appended hereto faithfully and dutifully.

Name of Missionary Kid _____
                        _____
                        _____
                        _____

Signed:

Girls in Action group from _____ Baptist Church, _____, TN.

Witness:_____
Date_____

Adoption Certificate

GIRLS IN ACTION of the Tennessee Woman's Missionary Union

This certifies that the Girls in Action of _____ Baptist Church

have officially adopted _____ as their own

Missionary Kid for the period of one year beginning on this date _____

and going through _____ .

In witness thereof the said Girls in Action
of Tennessee Woman's Missionary Union has
caused this Certificate to be signed and duly
authorized.

_____
Director

By-Laws of the Organization "Cousins"

NAME:

The name of this organization shall be "Cousins."

PURPOSE:

To provide fellowship and mutual support for sons and daughters of missionaries (here after referred to as "MKs").

MEMBERSHIP:

(1) This organization shall be open to OBU students whose parents are serving or have served as either home or foreign missionaries.

(2) Membership shall also be extended to other MKs or former MKs and their spouses who reside in Oklahoma.

SPONSOR:

The faculty sponsor shall be elected annually by the organization.

HONORARY SPONSORS:

The organization shall elect honorary sponsors as the members so desire.

ORGANIZATIONAL STRUCTURE:

(1) The organization shall elect annually an executive committee (EC) of seven members.

(2) The EC shall be responsible for the planning and promotion of the activities of the organization.

(3) The EC shall be responsible for its own internal organization.

(4) The EC shall meet monthly.

(5) Meetings of the EC shall be open to any member.

AMENDMENTS:

This constitution shall be amended by a three-fourths majority vote of the EC.

American Colleges and Universities Attended by MKs

ALABAMA

Auburn University, Auburn, AL 36830
Judson College, Marion, AL 36756
Mobile College, Mobile, AL 36613
Samford University, Birmingham, AL 35209
University of Alabama Medical School, Birmingham, AL 35294
University of Alabama, Huntsville, AL 35805
University of Montevallo, Montevallo, AL 35515
Wallace State Community College, Hanceville, AL 35077

ARIZONA

Grand Canyon College, 3300 Camelback Rd., Phoenix, AZ 85017
Prima Community College, West Anklam Rd., Tucson, AZ 85709
University of Arizona, Tucson, AZ 85721

ARKANSAS

Ouachita Baptist University, Arkadelphia, AR 71923
Henderson State University, Arkadelphia, AR 71923
University of Arkansas, Fayetteville, AR 72701
University of Arkansas, Little Rock, AR 72204

CALIFORNIA

Allan Hancock College, Santa Maria, CA 93454
Azusa Pacific College, Azusa, CA 91702
Biola College, La Mirada, CA 90639
Cabrillo Community College, Aptos, CA 94507
California State University, Fresno, CA 93740
La Verne College, La Verne, CA 91750
University of California, Berkeley, CA 94719
College of Redwoods, Eureka, CA 95501
Westmont College, 955 La Paz Rd., Santa Barbara, CA 93108

COLORADO

Community College of Denver, CO 80204
Denver Institute of Technology, 7350 N. Broadway, Denver, CO 80221
U.S. Air Force Academy
Western State College, Gunnison, CO 81230

CONNECTICUT

Wesleyan College, Middletown, CT 06457

DISTRICT OF Columbia

The American University, Washington, DC 20016

FLORIDA

Edison Community College, Ft. Myers, FL 33901
Florida State University, Tallahassee, FL 32306
Palm Beach Atlantic College, West Palm Beach, FL 33401
Pensacola Junior College, Pensacola, FL 32504
Santa Fe Community College, Gainesville, FL 32601
Stetson University, DeLand, FL 32720
University of Florida, Gainesville, FL 32601
University of South Florida, Tampa, FL 33620
University of West Florida, Pensacola, FL 32504
Warner Southern College, Lake Wales, FL 33853

GEORGIA

Clayton Junior College, Morrow, GA 30260
Emory University, Atlanta, GA 30322
Georgia Baptist Hospital School of Nursing, 300 Blvd., NE, Atlanta,
GA 30312
Georgia College, Milledgeville, GA 31601
Georgia Institute of Technology, Atlanta, GA 30332
Georgia Southern College, Statesboro, GA 30458
Georgia State University, Atlanta, GA 30303
Hall School of Nursing, Gainesville, GA 30501
LaGrange College, LaGrange, GA 30240
Medical College of Georgia, Augusta, GA 30909
Mercer University, Macon, GA 31207
Shorter College, Rome, GA 30161
University of Georgia, Athens, GA 30601
Valdosta State College, Valdosta, GA 31601
West Georgia College, Carrollton, GA 30117

ILLINOIS

Southern Illinois University, Carbondale, IL 62901
Wheaton College, Wheaton IL 60187

INDIANA

Indiana State University, Terre Haute, IN 47808
Indiana University, Bloomington, IN 47401
Purdue University, West Lafayette, IN 47907

KANSAS

Garden City Community College, Garden City, KS 67846
Ottawa University, Ottawa, KS 66067

KENTUCKY

Berea College, Berea, KY 40403
Campbellsville College, Campbellsville, KY 42718
Cumberland College, Williamsburg, KY 40769
Georgetown College, Gerogetown, KY 40769
Morehead State University, Morehead, KY 40351
Murray University, Murray, KY 42071
Spalding College, Louisville, KY 40203
University of Kentucky, Lexington, KY 40506
University of Louisville, Louisville, KY 40208
Western Kentucky University, Bowling Green, KY 42101

LOUISIANA

Louisiana College, Pineville, LA 71360
Louisiana State University, Baton Rouge, LA 70893
Louisiana Technological University, Ruston, LA
Northeast Louisiana University, Monroe, LA 71203

MARYLAND

Johns Hopkins University, Baltimore, MD 21218

MASSACHUSETTS

Massachusetts Institute of Technology, Cambridge MA 02139
Tufts University, Medford, MA 02155

MISSISSIPPI

Blue Mountain College, Blue Mountain, MS 38610
Hinds Junior College, Raymond, MS 39154
Mississippi College, Clinton, MS 39058
Mississippi State University, Storkville, MS 39762
University of Southern Mississippi, Hattiesburg, MS 39401
William Carey College, Hattiesburg, MS 39401

MISSOURI

Maple Woods College, Kansas City, MO 64156
Missouri Southern State College, Joplin, MO 64801
School of the Ozarks, Point Lookout, MO 65726
Southwest Baptist College, Bolivar, MO 65613
William Jewell College, Liberty, MO 64068

MONTANA

University of Montana, Missoula, MT 59801

NEW MEXICO

New Mexico State University, Las Cruces, NM 88003
University of New Mexico, Albuquerque, NM 87106

NORTH CAROLINA

Appalachia State University, Boone, NC 28607
Campbell College, Buies Creek, NC 27506
Duke University School of Medicine, Durham NC 27710
East Carolina University, Greenville, NC 27834
Gardner-Webb College, Boiling Springs, NC 28017
Mars Hill College, NC 28754
Meredith College, Raleigh, NC 27611
Montreat-Anderson College, Montreat, NC 28757
Penland School of Crafts, Penland, NC 28765
St. Andrews Presbyterian College, Laurinburg, NC 28352
University of North Carolina at Chapel Hill, Chapel Hill, NC 27514
University of North Carolina, Charlotte, NC 28213
University of North Carolina, Greenville, NC 27412
Wake Forest University, Winston-Salem, NC 27109
Warren Wilson College, Swannanoa, NC 28778
Wingate College, Wingate, NC 28174

OHIO

Denison University, Granville, OH 43023
Kent State University, Kent, OH 44240

OKLAHOMA

Carl Albert Junior College, Poteau, OK 74953
Central State University, Edmond, OK 73034
Northeastern Oklahoma State University, Tahlequah, OK 74464
Oklahoma Baptist University, Shawnee, OK 74801

Oklahoma State University, Stillwater, OK 74074
University of Oklahoma, Norman, OK 73069

PENNSYLVANIA

University of Pennsylvania, Philadelphia, PA 19174

SOUTH CAROLINA

Anderson College, Anderson, SC 29621
Bob Jones University, Greenville, SC 29614
College of Charleston, Charleston, SC 29401
Converse College, Spartanburg, SC 29301
Erskine College, Due West, SC 29639
Furman University, Greenville, SC 29613
University of South Carolina, Columbia, SC 29208
Winthrop College, Rock Hill, SC 29733
Wofford College, Spartanburg, SC 29301

TENNESSEE

Austin Peay State University, Clarksville, TN 37040
Belmont College, Nashville, TN 37203
Carson-Newman College, Jefferson City, TN 37760
East Tennessee State University, Johnson City, TN 37601
Middle Tennessee State University, Murfreesboro, TN 37130
Milligan College, Johnson City, TN 37659
Union University, Jackson, TN 38301
University of Tennessee Center of Health Sciences, Memphis, TN 38163
University of Tennessee, Knoxville, TN 37916
Vanderbilt University, Nashville, TN 37240

TEXAS

Abilene Christian University, Abilene, TX 79601
Baylor University, Waco, TX 76703
Baylor College of Medicine, Houston, TX 77030
Cisco Junior College, Abilene, TX 76437
Dallas Baptist College, Dallas, TX 75211
East Texas Baptist College, Marshall, TX 75670
East Texas State University, Commerce, TX 75668
Hardin-Simmons University, Abilene, TX 79601
Houston Baptist University, Houston, TX 77036
Howard Payne University, Brownwood, TX 76801
LeTourneau College, Longview, TX 75601
Mary Hardin-Baylor College, Belton, TX 76513

McLennan Community College, Waco, TX 76708
Midwestern State University, Wichita Falls, TX 76308
Mountain View Junior College, Dallas, TX 75211
North Texas State University, Denton, TX 76203
Odessa College, Odessa, TX 79761
Rice University, Houston, TX 77001
Southern Methodist University, Dallas, TX 75275
Southwest Texas STate University, San Marcos, TX 78666
Texas A & M University, College Station, TX 77840
Stephen F. Austin State University, Nacogodoches, TX 75962
Texas Christian University, Fort Worth, TX 76129
Texas State Technical Institute, Sweetwater, TX 79556
Texas State Technical Institute, James Connally Campus, Waco, TX 76703
Texas Technological University, Lubbock, TX 79409
Tyler Junior College, Tyler, TX 75701
University of Houston, Houston, TX 77004
University of Texas, Arlington, TX 76010
University of Texas, Austin, TX 78701
University of Texas, El Paso, TX 79968
Wayland Baptist College, Plainview, TX 79072
West Texas State University, Canyon, TX 79015

VIRGINIA

College of William & Mary, Williamsburg, VA 23185
Ferrum College, Ferrum, VA 24088
Hollins College, Hollins, VA 24020
Medical College of Virginia, Richmond, VA 23298
University of Richmond, Richmond, VA 23173
University of Virginia, Charlottesville, VA 22903
Virginia Polytechnic Institute & State University, Blacksburg, VA 24061
Westhampton College, Richmond, VA 23173

WASHINGTON

Washington State University, Pullman, WA 99163

WEST VIRGINIA

Alderson-Broaddus College, Philippi, WV 26416

Glossary

Glossary

The Baptist Brotherhood Commission. A missions organization of the Southern Baptist Convention located at 1548 Poplar Avenue, Memphis, Tennessee 38104. Their primary responsibility is the enlistment of Baptist men and boys for inspiration and instruction in the world mission task of the Convention.

Candidate. One who is involved in the appointment process as a missionary to be commissioned.

Candidate consultant. One of five people in the Personnel Selection Department who are primarily responsible for the enlistment, nurture, evaluation, and selection of career missionaries. He is also known as a "regional representative."

Dissertation. An original, well-researched and written work done under the guidance of one or more professors and concerned with some aspect of the student's major field of study.

Family Life Consultant, Healthy Family Ministries. In 1971, the FMB appointed Truman S. Smith to be the Missionary Family Consultant, now known as the Family Consultant, Healthy Family Ministries. He had previously served with the board since 1964 as an associate secretary in the Department of Missionary Personnel. He plans and directs the Thanksgiving MK Retreat each year for college freshmen; visits college campuses; plans family emphases throughout the world; meets with parents and missionaries at Foreign Mission Week held annually at Glorieta, New Mexico, and Ridgecrest, North Carolina, and assists in every way possible to solve problems occuring in missionary families.

FMB. The Foreign Mission Board of the Southern Baptist Convention located in Richmond, Virginia, Box 6597, 23230.

Furlough options. The availability of various plans for returning to the United States from the missionary's foreign field of service dependent upon how long he has served, for example:

Length of Service	Length of Furlough
2 years	2 months
2½ years	3 months
3 years	6 months
3½ years	9 months
4 years	12 months
5 years	14 months

Human Resources Subcommittee. A committee of board members with the responsibility of reviewing the candidate's application, sense of calling, and anticipated assignment.

Journeyman. One of five categories of missionary service with the Foreign Mission Board, SBC, open to college graduates age twenty-six and under for a two-year term of service with a specific job assignment.

Manual for Missionaries. A publication by the Office of Overseas Operations of the Foreign Mission Board, SBC, to provide each missionary with a ready reference to Board policy regarding personal matters in missionary support and to describe the relationships of each missionary to the mission and to the Foreign Mission Board staff. Policy is always subject to change.

Margaret Fund Scholarship. $625 is sent each semester ($1,250 per year) to be credited to the account of the MK (Southern Baptist) in college. This provision is for four years, a total of $5,000. The Margaret Fund grant is $750 for one year of graduate study. In the event that the study is done in a Southern Baptist seminary, $750 each year up to three years is provided.

Missionary associate. Another of the five categories of missionary service open to Southern Baptists age thirty-five to sixty for a four-year term of service in an English language assignment.

MK. A term of unknown origin meaning "missionary kid." Its origins in print can be traced as far back as the early 1940s in a publication by Marjorie Moore Armstrong entitled "The Little Commission." It is thought to have been in use prior to that time.

Mission station. All Southern Baptist missionaries within a given geographical location such as a city or state.

MOC. Missionary Orientation Center. Newly located on a 230-acre tract near Richmond, Virginia, the Orientation Center holds a time of preparing missionaries lasting eight weeks. Previously, orientation had been held at Calloway Gardens, Georgia (1969-1982).

Nationals. Those residents of the foreign country who compose the denomination.

Personal histories. A concise in-depth look at the candidate and his personal background written by the same in order that an in-depth relationship might be established as the candidate moves through the appointment process.

Personnel Selection Department. The department of the Foreign Mission Board, SBC, consisting of nine members, five of which are candidate consultants. The department responds to contacts from those interested in possible mission service, helps them to discern God's will, and assists those pursuing a career in missions through the appointment process.

Regional representative. (See candidate consultant.)

Surveys. Six surveys were made use of in the writing of this manuscript. In order to better distinguish between them you will find listed below the name of the survey, the date it was taken, and who it surveyed (all surveys were taken by this author unless otherwise identified), and the total surveyed:

Survey Name	Date	Population Surveyed
Dissertation Survey	04/29/78	All Margaret Fund MKs in US colleges and universities (578 total)
South Brazil	07/03/79	All missionary pa-

Parents Survey		rents (89 total)
Worldwide Survey	09/11/80	All missionary parents throughout the world (1,165 total)
MK Weekend Survey	11/22-25/79	All MKs at the annual MK weekend (131 total)
Laura Sprinkle Lane Survey	Fall/76	Random sample of MKs in colleges throughout the US (50 total)
Sophia Regina Gomes Survey	04/76	MKs attending colleges and universities in North and South Carolina (40 total)

WMU. The Woman's Missionary Union of the Southern Baptist Convention, Highway 280 East, 100 Missionary Ridge, P.O. Box C-10, Birmingham, Alabama 35243-2798.

Bibliography

Bibliography

BOOKS

Collins, Majorie A. *Manual for Accepted Missionary Candidates.* South Pasadena, CA: William Carey Library, 1972.

Combs, Arthur W. and Snygg, Donald. *Individual Behavior.* New York: Harper and Row, 1959.

Conger, John J. *Adolescence and Youth.* New York: Harper and Row, 1973.

Drakeford, John W. *Integrity Therapy.* Nashville: Broadman Press, 1967.

Elkind, David. *The Hurried Child: Growing Up Too Fast Too Soon.* Reading, Massachusetts: Addison-Wesley Publishing Company, 1981.

Erikson, G. H. *Identity: Youth and Crisis.* New York: Norton Co., 1968.

Frank, Lawrence K. "Cultural Control and Physiological Autonomy." In *Personality in Nature, Society and Culture.* Edited by Clyde Kluckhohn, Henry A. Murray and David M. Schneider. New York: Alfred A. Knopf, 1967.

Freeman, Frank S. *Theory and Practice of Psychological Testing,* 3 ed. New York: Holt, Rinehart and Winston, 1962.

Kemp, Charles F. *Counseling with College Students.* Englewood Cliffs: Prentice-Hall, 1964.

Lockerbie, D. Bruce. *Education of Missionary's Children: The Neglected Dimension of World Missions.* South Pasadena, Cal.: William Carey Library, 1976.

Marshall, Catherine. *Beyond Our Selves.* New York: McGraw-Hill Book Company, Inc., 1959.

Peck, Robert F. "Student Mental Health: The Range of Personality Patterns in a College Population." In *Personality Factors on the College Campus.* Edited by Robert T. Sutherland, Wayne H. Holtzman, Earl A. Koile, and Bert Kruger Smith. Austin, Texas: The Hogg Foundation for Mental Health, 1962.

Rahe, Richard. "Are You Under Pressure and Can You Cope?" In *Feel Younger, Live Longer.* Edited by Jack Tresidder. Chicago: Rand McNally, 1976.

Swenson, Wendell M., Pearson, John S., and Osborne, David. *An MMPI Source Book.* Minneapolis: University of Minnesota Press, 1973.

Wilson, Edmund. *The Wound and the Bow.* New York: Oxford University Press, 1965.

CORRESPONDENCE AND INTERVIEWS

Crim to Viser, 9 March 1983.
Davis to Viser, 1 October 1981.
Davis to Viser, 2 February 1983.
Dowler to Viser, 28 March 1983.
Elliott to Viser, 28 March 1983.
Fowler to Viser, 2 November 1981.
Gilpin to Viser, 25 February 1983.
Holland to Viser, 12 October 1983.
Krushwitz to Viser, 24 January 1983.
Krushwitz to Viser, 27 January 1983.
Lawrence to Viser, 1 March 1983.
Moore to Viser, 21 December 1981.
Mullendore to Viser, 10 March 1983.
Pitman to Viser, 26 April 1983.
Rader to Viser, 4 April 1983.
Reavis to Viser, 12 February 1981.
Reid to Viser, 23 February 1983.
Smith to E. V. May, Jr., 19 September 1972.
Smith to Tina Block Ediger, 1 May 1979.

MANUSCRIPTS

Guyner, Delmer R. "A Study of Relationships Between Selected Personality Factors and Personal Adjustment of Overseas Personnel." Unpublished EdD dissertation, North Texas State University, 1975.

Krajewski, Frank R. "A Study of the Relationship of an Overseas-experienced Population Based on Sponsorship of Parent and Subsequent Academic Adjustment to College in the United States." Unpublished PhD dissertation, Michigan State University, 1969.

Viser, William C. "A Psychological Profile of Missionary Children in College and the Relationship of Intense Group Therapy to Weekly Group Therapy in the Treatment of Personality Problems as Reflected by the Minnesota Multiphasic Personality Inventory." Unpublished EdD dissertation, Southwestern Baptist Theological Seminary, 1978.

NEWSPAPERS

"MKs Reflect Upon MK Life." *Mississippi Collegian.* October 1974.

"Question of the Week." *Japan Times*, 29 August 1976.

"Question of the Week." *Japan Times*, 5 September 1976.

" 'Third Culture Kids' Feel Like Foreigners in Their Own Country." *Richmond-Times Dispatch*, 8 December 1974.

PAMPHLETS

"The Appointment Process." Mimeographed. Richmond: Department of Personnel, Foreign Mission Board, SBC, 1980.

"Madge Truex Fund." Mimeographed. Jefferson City, Missouri: Woman's Missionary Union of the Missouri Baptist Convention, 1982.

OTHER MIMEOGRAPHED MATERIAL

"Education of MKs." Mimeographed. Richmond: Department of Orientation and Development, Foreign Mission Board, SBC, n.d.

"Instructions for Writing Your Personal History." Mimeographed. Richmond: Department of Personnel, Foreign Mission Board, SBC, n.d.

"Manual for Missionaries." Mimeographed. Richmond: Office of Overseas Operations, Foreign Mission Board, SBC, n.d.

"Margaret Fund Students, Spring Semester, 1980." Mimeographed. Richmond: Office of Administration, Foreign Mission Board, SBC, 1980.

"Ministering to Missionaries and Their Families." Gene and Ann Pitman. Mimeographed. Corpus Christi, Texas: Texas Woman's Missionary Union Annual Meeting, 1982.

"Physician's Physical Examination Form for Children." Richmond: Department of the Medical Consultant, Foreign Mission Board, SBC, 1980.

PERIODICALS AND JOURNALS

Bier, William C. "A Modified Form of the Minnesota Multiphasic Personality Inventory for Religious Personnel." *Theological Education,* 1971:3.

Cahen, Susan S. "Classrooms: A Wide Variety." *The Commission,* August 1971:9.

Cox, Ted. "Missionary Milestones: Family Separation." *Royal Service,* August 1976:11.

Cresswell, Mike. "He's Back in the Light." *The Commission,* September 1981:12-17.

Cummins, Betty. "Growing Up in East Africa." *The Commission,* July 1976:39.

Downs, Ray F. "A Look at the Third Culture Child." *The Japan Christian Quarterly,* Spring 1976:67-68.

Fowler, Franklin. "The Third World Culture of the MK." *The Commission,* December 1970:1-3.

Fowler, Ruth. "Just a Title." *The Commission,* April 1975:18.

Fowler, Ruth. "The MK Perspective: Growing Up Overseas." *Contempo,* July 1976:10-11.

Gleason, Thomas P. "The Overseas-Experienced American

Adolescent and Patterns of Worldmindedness." *Adolescents,* Winter 1973:486.

Hill, Jonnie. "An MK's Search for Home." *Foreign Missionary Intercom,* November 1981:2.

Hill, M. E. "The Separation Syndrome." *The Commission,* January 1975:30.

Howell, Charles H. "Family Shock." *The Commission,* November 1974:8.

Hsieh, Theodore. "Missionary Family Behavior, Dissonance and Children's Career Decision." *Journal of Psychology and Theology,* Summer 1976:226.

Jameson, Norman. " 'Missionary Kids' Feel God Calling Home." *Baptist Standard,* 13 April 1983:20.

Kines, Linda B. "The Shock of Coming Home." *The Commission,* August 1971:12.

Lewis, Roy F. "The Greatest Sacrifice." *The Commission,* January 1975:12.

Lockard, Susi. "Partners in Preparation." *The Commission,* February 1978:1.

Lockard, W. David. "MKs—Call Them Winners." *Accent,* June 1975:6.

Lockerbie, Donny. "Missionary Kids Are Just Kids." *Eternity,* March 1976:23.

Longest, Susan S. "I Am An MK." *Foreign Missionary Intercom,* January 1982:3.

McClellan, "The Anguishes of the Missionary." *The Baptist Program,* October 1977:6.

McKay, Marie. "God Bless the Missionaries." *Royal Service,* April 1983:40-41.

Menzies, Marina. "Top Ten Prayer Needs." *The Commission,* December 1981:29.

Miley, Lorene. "God Bless Our Missionaries . . . And Help the MKs Too." *Heartbeat,* September-October 1971:3.

O'Brien, Robert. "Looking Ahead." *The Commission,* February-March 1983:5.

Parkman, Leslie. "Switching From Rice to French Fries." *Contempo*, January 1977:4.

Ryals, Nancy Blevins. "Missionary Families." *Royal Service*, January 1977:21.

Shields, Teresa. "They Share a Common Heritage." *The Commission*, March 1976:10.

Skelton, Martha. "Missionary Families: Some Stresses and Strengths." *The Commission*, December 1981:8.

Skelton, Martha. " 'Mom, I'm Watching History,' MK Says." *The Commission*, December 1981:13.

Smith, Truman S. "Missionary Families: Human and Heroic." *Home Life*, June 1980:28-29.

Smith, Truman S. "Open Letter to High School MKs." *Foreign Missionary Intercom*, April 1981:1.

Smith, Kendra. "MK Letters." *Accent*, April 1975:21.

Stamps, Stanley D. "MK Roots." *The Commission*, January 1975:6.

Steele, Kathy. "Naming Some Stresses." *The Commission*, December 1981:9.

Stewart David. "To the Larger Family." *The Commission*, January 1975:9.

Swadley, Elizabeth. "MKs Away from Home." *Royal Service*, January 1977:27.

Tanner, William C. "Strictly Personal for Parents of MKs."

Turner, Mary Jane Welch. "Contempo Interview I: Louis R. Cobbs, Billy Krushwitz and Don Reavis." *Contempo*, March 1980:14.

Ward, Mary Ann. "Family Weekend Away from Home." *Royal Service*, November 1974:9.

Ward, Mary Ann. "MK Letters." *Accent*, July 1975:27.

Wakefield, Delcie. "The Versatile 'Homemaker.' " *The Commission*, November 1974:8.

Webb, Leland. "Ceremony at 15." *The Commission*, August 1971:21.

Webb, Leland and Kelly, Dora. "Finding Her Role." *The Commission*, November 1974:5.

Werkman, Sidney L. "Hazards of Rearing Children in Foreign Countries." *American Journal of Psychiatry*, February 1972:-107.

Willmon, Jeannine. "An MK Comes Home." *The Commission*, August 1971:23.

RESEARCH

Gomes, Sophia Regina. "Research on Missionary Kids." Mimeographed. Gardner-Webb College, Boiling Springs, North Carolina, 1972.

Lane, Laura S. "Missionary Kids Share Their Feelings About Being MKs." Mimeographed. Carson-Newman College, Jefferson City, Tennessee, 1976.